LUXURY TRAINS

LUXURY TRAINS

edited by Eva Marín

teNeues

Editor:	Eva Marín
Text:	Priya Bhansali, Victoria See, E. Marín
Editor in chief:	Inma Alavedra
Layout & Prepress	S. García
Translation:	Mechthild Barth, Anne Winterling (German)
	Carlo Prosperi, Simona Mambrini (Italian)
	Julie Meyers (French)
	Victoria See, Lauren Tejada (English)

Published by teNeues Publishing Group

teNeues Verlag GmbH + Co. KG
Am Selder 37, 47906 Kempen, Germany
Tel.: 0049-(0)2152-916-0, Fax: 0049-(0)2152-916-111
e-mail: books@teneues.de

Press department: Andrea Rehn
Tel.: 0049-(0)2152-916-202
e-mail: arehn@teneues.de

teNeues Publishing Company
16 West 22nd Street, New York, N.Y. 10010, USA
Tel.: 001-212-627-9090, Fax: 001-212-627-9511

teNeues Publishing UK Ltd.
P.O. Box 402, West Byfleet, KT14 7ZF, Great Britain
Tel.: 0044-1932-4035-09, Fax: 0044-1932-4035-14

teNeues France S.A.R.L.
93, rue Bannier, 45000 Orléans, France
Tel.: 0033-2-3854-1071, Fax: 0033-2-3862-5340

www.teneues.com

ISBN: 978-3-8327-9267-1

Printed in Italy

Bibliographic information published by the Deutsche Nationalbibliothek.
The Deutsche Nationalbibliothek lists this publication in the Deutsche Nationalbibliografie;
detailed bibliographic data are available in the Internet at http://dnb.d-nb.de.

CONTENTS

INTRODUCTION

Two events marked the beginning of the history of luxury trains: a sleepless night for an industrial pioneer, George Pullman, and the death of a president, Abraham Lincoln. Despite the fact that sleeping cars have existed in the United States since 1830, their accommodations and comfort left a great deal to be desired. George Pullman, a successful American industrialist, experienced it for himself during a night trip that traveled from Buffalo, NY to Westfield, NY in 1857. He did not sleep a wink the entire night and used those sleepless hours to design what would become the first luxury trains. However, the rail companies rejected his proposal at that time.

Almost a decade later, in May of 1865, Pullman and his trains became famous throughout the country as they formed part of Lincoln's funeral. The Pullman Palace Car, as its creator called it, captured the essence of what was soon to come in the turning point for the train. It made and served exquisite dishes on board in a refined atmosphere with a décor that was elegant, lavish, and adorned with luxurious materials.

Today, luxury trains continue to be like hotels on wheels. With impeccable service, they pay attention to every last detail in order to make the trip itself as pleasing and significant—sometimes even more so—as the destination. Those that choose these means of transportation will undoubtedly enjoy a truly captivating experience, whether going to one of the mythical routes of old Europe, landmarks within the American continent, or exotic Asian or African destinations.

The luxury train sector is booming, evident in the fact that it continues to create new routes and trains of this kind every year, and in many occasions train reservations have to be made more than a year in advance. Beyond discovering places inch-by-inch that are at times inaccessible by any other way, the traveler also completely immerses himself in a world of opulence in all respects.

Another train travel alternative, and by no means less luxurious, are the modern trains that often combine leisure and business, some of which are high speed. With much more current line designs, they offer all types of services just as much for professionals—who can work or hold meetings aboard—as for tourists. These trains are fast, comfortable and transport passengers to the heart of the city or to the highest peaks of the Alps or those in Tibet, which are about three miles high.

Luxury Trains shows some of the most spectacular train stations on the planet and provides images of trains from the latest generation and the routes of some of the most mythical trains in the world. On a trip through time—illustrated with images of the period—one-by-one the best trains of today are visited inside and out. A door is opened to reveal trains' restaurants, suites draped with the most luxurious fabrics, Victorian bathtubs, gold faucets, period furniture made of fine wood, and linen sheets. We are shown everything from the delicacies prepared by French chefs to the uniforms worn by the staff who take care of each detail such as serving tea each afternoon to every compartment. Ultimately, what makes these trains more than just a means of transportation is the sophisticated pleasure of the trip itself, as C.P. Cavafis describes in his poem Ithaca, "Ithaca has given you the beautiful voyage. Without her you would have never set out on the road."

Blue Train

EINLEITUNG

Zwei Ereignisse stehen am Beginn des Luxuszuges: eine schlaflose Nacht für den Industriepionier George Pullman und der Tod des amerikanischen Präsidenten Abraham Lincoln. Auch wenn bereits seit 1830 in den USA Schlafwagen existierten, so ließen sie doch hinsichtlich ihrer Unterbringungsmöglichkeiten und Bequemlichkeit viel zu wünschen übrig. George Pullman, ein erfolgreicher amerikanischer Industrieller, erfuhr das am eigenen Leib, als er 1857 nachts mit dem Zug von Buffalo/NY nach Westfield/NY reiste. Die ganze Zeit über tat er kein Auge zu, nutzte aber die schlaflosen Stunden, um den ersten Luxuszug der Welt zu entwerfen. Jedoch lehnten die Bahngesellschaften seinen Entwurf zu dieser Zeit ab.

Als Pullman und sein Zug allerdings beinahe ein Jahrzehnt später im Mai 1865 Lincolns Begräbnis begleiteten, wurden sie im ganzen Land berühmt. Der Pullman Palace Car, wie sein Erfinder ihn nannte, vereinte zum ersten Mal all das in sich, was einen Luxuszug ausmachen sollte. In einem raffinierten Ambiente und einem eleganten, üppigen, mit wertvollen Materialien geschmückten Interieur wurden exquisite Gerichte serviert, die an Bord zubereitet wurden.

Auch heute noch erinnern Luxuszüge an Hotels auf Schienen. Beim tadellosen Service wird auf jedes kleinste Detail geachtet, um die Reise genauso angenehm und außergewöhnlich wie das Reiseziel selbst zu gestalten – und manchmal sogar noch angenehmer und außergewöhnlicher. Wer diese Art der Fortbewegung wählt, wird eine fesselnde Erfahrung machen, ob nun auf einer der mythischen Routen durch Europa, auf einer Reise zu den Sehenswürdigkeiten des amerikanischen Kontinents oder in ein exotisches asiatisches oder afrikanisches Land.

Die Branche der Luxuszüge boomt. So werden jedes Jahr neue Routen und Züge entwickelt, und oftmals muss man bereits mehr als ein Jahr im Voraus buchen. Der Reisende vermag dabei nicht nur Orte zu entdecken, die manchmal nicht anders zugänglich wären, sondern er kann auch vollkommen in eine Welt des Überflusses eintauchen.

Eine andere, nicht weniger luxuriöse Möglichkeit, mit der Bahn zu fahren, sind die modernen Züge, die sowohl für Freizeitangebote als auch für Geschäftsreisen genutzt werden können – und das oft in Höchstgeschwindigkeit. In einem modernen Stil gehalten, bieten sie alle Arten von Service sowohl für Geschäftsleute, die an Bord arbeiten oder Meetings abhalten können, als auch für Touristen an. Die Züge sind schnell, bequem und bringen den Reisenden ins Zentrum einer Stadt, auf die höchsten Gipfel der Alpen oder auch auf die von Tibet, von denen manche über 5000 Meter in die Höhe ragen.

Luxury Trains präsentiert einige der spektakulärsten Bahnhöfe der Welt, Bilder der neuesten Züge und die Bahnrouten für einige der mythischsten Züge der Erde. Auf einer Reise durch die Zeit – illustriert mit Darstellungen aus der jeweiligen Ära – betrachten wir die besten Züge, die es heutzutage gibt. Eine Tür öffnet sich für uns zu den Bordrestaurants, den mit luxuriösen Stoffen ausgestatteten Suiten, mit viktorianischen Badewannen, goldenen Wasserhähnen, antiken Möbeln aus feinstem Holz und echter Leinenbettwäsche. Uns wird alles gezeigt – angefangen von den Delikatessen französischer Chefköche bis hin zu den Uniformen der Angestellten, die sich um jedes kleine Detail kümmern, wie das Servieren des Nachmittagstees in jedem einzelnen Abteil. Was diese Züge jedoch zu mehr als einem bloßen Transportmittel macht, ist das niveauvolle Vergnügen der Reise selbst – wie das C. P. Cavafis in seinem Gedicht Ithaca beschreibt: „Ithaca hat dir eine wunderbare Fahrt beschert. Ohne Ithaca hättest du dich niemals aufgemacht."

Golden Eagle

INTRODUCTION

Deux évènements marquent le commencement de l'histoire des trains de luxe. La nuit blanche d'un industriel pionnier, George Pullman et la mort d'Abraham Lincoln. Les wagons-lits existent aux États-Unis depuis 1830 mais leurs prestations et leur confort ne sont pas à encore à la hauteur. George Pullman, un industriel américain prospère, en fit l'expérience lors d'un voyage de nuit entre Buffalo et Westfield (New York) en 1857. Il ne ferma pas l'œil de la nuit et profita de ces heures perdues pour concevoir ce qui seraient les premiers wagons de luxe. Mais les compagnies ferroviaires refuseront alors sa proposition.

Une décennie plus tard, en mai 1865, son train faisant partie des funérailles d'Abraham Lincoln, Pullman et ses wagons sont couronnés de succès dans tout le pays. Le Pullman Palace Car, ainsi nommé par leur créateur – littéralement « wagon palace » –, reprend l'esprit de ce que seront plus tard les croisières en train. Y sont élaborés et servis des plats fins dans une ambiance distinguée, une décoration élégante et somptueuse, riche en matériels nobles.

Les trains de luxe continuent d'être aujourd'hui de véritables hôtels sur roues. Un service de qualité et une attention portée au moindre détail fait du voyage une expérience aussi importante et agréable ou même parfois plus que la destination. Ceux choisissant ce moyen de transport désirent jouir de luxe et de confort lors de leur voyage, que ce soient le long des routes mythiques de la vieille Europe, des vastes étendues du continent américains ou des destinations exotiques asiatiques ou africaines.

C'est un secteur en plein essor. La création incessante de nouvelles routes et trains de cette caractéristique chaque année et les réservations devant se faire souvent une année à l'avance le démontrent. Au-delà de la découverte pied à pied de territoires souvent inaccessibles d'une autre manière, le voyageur est immergé dans un monde d'opulence.

Une autre alternative, non moins luxueuse, pour voyager en train, dans laquelle se conjuguent souvent loisirs et affaires reste celle des trains modernes, pour certains à grande vitesse. Avec un design beaucoup plus actuel, ils offrent tous les types de services aussi bien pour hommes d'affaires – les permettant travailler à bord et organiser des réunions – que pour touristes. Ils sont rapides, confortables et nous conduisent jusqu'au centre des villes ou aux cimes les plus hautes du Tibet à 5000 mètres d'altitude, ou des Alpes.

Luxury Trains présente une sélection de gares les plus spectaculaires de la planète et nous transporte à travers d'images dans les trains dernière génération et par les routes des trains les plus mythiques du monde. Dans un voyage à travers le temps – illustrés par des images d'époques – et l'espace, cet ouvrage visite un à un, de l'intérieur comme de l'extérieur les meilleurs trains d'aujourd'hui. Il ouvre les portes de ses voitures-restaurants, de ses suites revêtues d'étoffes les plus précieuses, ses baignoires victoriennes, ses robinetteries en or, ses meubles d'époque en bois nobles et ses draps de lin. Il offre une vision complète des services proposés, des délices préparés par les grands chefs français jusqu'aux uniformes du personnel soignant chaque détail, portant le thé chaque après-midi dans les compartiments. Finalement, il illustre les petites et grandes raisons qui font du train, plus qu'un moyen de transport, un plaisir sophistiqué, tel le voyage à Ithaque, du poème de C.P. Cavafis : ce qui enrichit le plus les voyageurs ce n'est pas tant Ithaque que le chemin : « Ithaque t'a donné le beau voyage : sans elle, tu ne te serais pas mis en route. »

Royal Canadian Pacific

INTRODUCCIÓN

Dos hechos marcaron el inicio de la historia de los trenes de lujo. La noche en vela de un industrial pionero, George Pullman y la muerte de un presidente, Abraham Lincoln. A pesar de que los coches cama existían desde 1830 en Estados Unidos, sus prestaciones y su confort dejaban mucho que desear. George Pullman, un próspero industrial americano, lo pudo comprobar en un viaje nocturno que realizó desde Buffalo a Westfield (New York) en 1857. No pegó ojo en toda la noche y aprovechó esas horas en blanco para diseñar los que serían los primeros vagones de lujo. Sin embargo las compañías ferroviarias rechazaron su propuesta por aquel entonces.

Casi una década más tarde, en mayo de 1865, Pullman y sus vagones cobraron fama en todo el país, puesto que su tren formó parte del funeral de Lincoln. El Pullman Palace Car, como los denominó su creador —literalmente "vagón palacio"—, recogía el espíritu de lo que serían en adelante los cruceros en tren. Se elaboraban y servían platos exquisitos a bordo en un ambiente refinado, con una decoración elegante, suntuosa y rica en materiales nobles.

Los trenes de lujo siguen siendo verdaderos hoteles sobre ruedas. Con un servicio impecable, ponen atención hasta en el último detalle para hacer que el viaje en sí sea tan importante y placentero, y en ocasiones incluso más que el destino. Aquellos que escogen este medio de transporte están apostando por deleitarse en el camino, ya sea siguiendo una de las míticas rutas de la vieja Europa, los parajes del continente americano o los exóticos destinos asiáticos o africanos.

Este es un sector en auge, como demuestra el hecho de que no cesen de crear nuevas rutas y trenes de estas características cada año y que en muchas ocasiones las reservas han de realizarse con más de un año de antelación. Más allá de descubrir palmo a palmo parajes en ocasiones inaccesibles de otro modo, el viajero se sumerge en todo un mundo de opulencia en todos los sentidos.

Otra alternativa, no menos lujosa, para viajar en tren, en la que a menudo se conjuga ocio y negocio son los trenes modernos, algunos de ellos de alta velocidad. Con diseños de líneas mucho más actuales, ofrecen todo tipo de servicios tanto para profesionales —pueden trabajar o mantener reuniones a bordo— como para turistas. Son rápidos confortables y conducen hasta el propio corazón de la ciudad o a las cimas más altas, en el Tibet a 5.000 metros de altura o en los Alpes.

Luxury Trains muestra algunas de las estaciones más espectaculares del planeta y nos transporta a través de imágenes por los trenes de última generación y por las rutas de algunos de los trenes más míticos del mundo. Mediante un viaje en el tiempo —ilustrado con imágenes de época— y en el espacio, visita uno a uno, por dentro y por fuera los mejores trenes en la actualidad. Abre una puerta a sus coches restaurante, suites vestidas con los tejidos más ricos, bañeras victorianas, griferías de oro, muebles de época de maderas nobles y sábanas de lino. Nos muestra desde las delicias que preparan los chefs franceses a los uniformes del personal que cuida cada detalle, como llevar el té cada tarde al compartimento. En definitiva ilustra los pequeños y grandes motivos que hacen del tren, más que un medio de transporte un sofisticado placer, como describe C.P. Cavafis en su poema Ítaca lo que enriquece más a los viajeros no es tanto Ítaca como el camino: "Itaca te ha dado un bello viaje de no ser por ella nunca te hubieras puesto en camino."

Le Train Bleu, Gare de Lyon, Paris

INTRODUZIONE

Due avvenimenti hanno segnato l'inizio dell'epopea dei treni di lusso: la notte in bianco di un pioniere dell'industria, George Pullman, e la morte di un presidente, Abramo Lincoln. Malgrado i vagoni letto esistessero negli Stati Uniti già dal 1830, il comfort e il livello delle prestazioni lasciavano molto a desiderare. George Pullman, imprenditore americano di successo, poté sperimentarlo in prima persona nel 1857, durante un viaggio notturno da Buffalo a Westfield, nello stato di New York. Pullman non riuscì a chiudere occhio tutta la notte ma approfittò delle ore insonni per progettare quelli che diventeranno i primi treni di lusso. Sul momento, tuttavia, le compagnie ferroviarie rifiutarono la sua proposta.

Quasi dieci anni dopo, nel maggio del 1865, Pullman e sui treni divennero famosi in tutto il paese per aver partecipato al corteo funebre di Lincoln. La Pullman Palace Car, "carrozza palazzo", come la chiamò il suo creatore, catturava lo spirito di quelle che sarebbero ben presto diventate vere e proprie crociere ferroviarie: a bordo venivano preparati piatti squisiti, serviti in un'atmosfera raffinata, tra arredi eleganti, sontuosi, realizzati in materiali di pregio.

Oggi, i treni di lusso continuano a essere hotel su ruote, il cui impeccabile servizio presta attenzione anche ai minimi dettagli pur di rendere il viaggio stesso piacevole e memorabile quanto la destinazione, se non di più. Che percorra una delle tratte leggendarie della vecchia Europa, che sia diretto ai principali luoghi di visita del continente americano o verso esotiche destinazioni in Africa o in Asia, chi sceglie questo mezzo di trasporto vivrà senza dubbio un'esperienza affascinante.

Il settore dei treni di lusso è in piena espansione, come si evince dai nuovi percorsi via via disponibili e dai treni di questa categoria prodotti ogni anno, tanto che spesso è necessario prenotare con mesi di anticipo. Oltre a scoprire palmo a palmo luoghi a volte inaccessibili con altri mezzi, il viaggiatore si immerge completamente in un mondo all'insegna dell'opulenza più sfrenata.

Una ulteriore alternativa di viaggio, e di certo non meno lussuosa, è offerta da treni moderni che spesso coniugano business e divertimento, alcuni dei quali ad alta velocità. Con linee e design più al passo con i tempi, questi mettono a disposizione un'amplissima gamma di servizi, tanto per i professionisti – che possono lavorare o tenere riunioni a bordo – quanto per i turisti. Sono treni veloci e comodi che conducono i passeggeri fin nel cuore della città o sulle vette più alte, dalle Alpi agli oltre 5000 metri delle montagne del Tibet.

Luxury Trains mostra alcune delle più straordinarie stazioni ferroviarie del mondo, accompagnandoci in un viaggio a bordo di carrozze di ultima generazione e su tratte percorse da treni ormai entrati nella leggenda. Un viaggio nel tempo – corredato da immagini d'epoca – e nello spazio, che ci permetterà di visitare, uno dopo l'altro, i migliori convogli oggi disponibili, aprendo le porte su ristoranti, suite addobbate con i tessuti più preziosi, vasche da bagno vittoriane, rubinetti in oro, lenzuola di lino e mobili d'epoca realizzati con i legni più pregiati. Ci mostrerà tutto, dalle prelibatezze preparate da chef francesi fino alle livree indossate da un personale attento a ogni minimo dettaglio, come il tè pomeridiano servito in ogni scompartimento. Ma ciò che rende questi treni molto più di un semplice mezzo di trasporto è il gusto stesso del viaggio, come ci ricorda il poeta C. P. Cavafis nella sua Itaca: "Itaca ti ha dato il bel viaggio, senza di lei mai ti saresti messo sulla strada".

Glacier Express

LUXURY
TRAIN
CRUISES

LUXURY TRAIN CRUISES

Luxury trains have provided travelers with a unique means of transportation for more than a century. They are often referred to as "hotels on wheels" as they embody the same extravagance found only in the most glamorous five-star hotel accommodations. This specialized luxury travel features endless amenities, attentive service, and fine dining for all guests to experience during their unforgettable journeys.

Luxuszüge bieten Reisenden seit über hundert Jahren eine einzigartige Form der Fortbewegung. Man bezeichnet sie oft als „Hotels auf Rädern", da sich in ihnen dieselbe Extravaganz wie in den luxuriösesten Fünf-Sterne-Hotels finden lässt. Zu dieser speziellen Form der Luxusreisen gehören zahlreiche Annehmlichkeiten, ein aufmerksamer Service und ausgezeichnetes Essen, so dass die Gäste unvergessliche Reiseerlebnisse mit nach Hause nehmen können.

Depuis plus d'un siècle, les trains de luxe offrent aux voyageurs un moyen unique et à part de transport. Souvent appelés « hôtels sur roues », ils présentent le même luxe que les hôtels cinq étoiles les plus élégants. Ces voyages spécialisés de luxe proposent une infinité d'agréments, un service attentif et des dîners raffinés à tous les invités pour que leur voyage reste inoubliable.

Los trenes de lujo han sido desde hace más de un siglo un medio de transporte único. Nos referimos a menudo a ellos como "hoteles sobre ruedas", ya que alcanzan niveles de lujo similares a los que podemos encontrar en los hoteles de cinco estrellas más glamurosos. Estos cruceros se caracterizan por ofrecer un sinfín de cuidados servicios y por las exquisitas comidas que los pasajeros pueden disfrutar durante viajes que resultan inolvidables.

Da centinaia di anni i treni di lusso offrono ai viaggiatori un mezzo di trasporto unico. Se ne parla spesso come di "hotel su ruote" perché fanno sfoggio dello stesso sfarzo che si può trovare solo nei più raffinati alberghi a cinque stelle. Questo esclusivo trasporto di lusso rende indimenticabile il viaggio, mettendo a disposizione di tutti gli ospiti infinite comodità, servizio personalizzato, cucina da gourmet.

page 16: Rovos Rail

right: British Pullman

VENICE SIMPLON

The vintage carriages of the Venice Simplon from the 1920s and 1930s offer an experience reminiscent of the romanticism and elegance of the era. Both the collection of original British Pullman cars and Wagons-Lits cars are used en route. Personal stewards and panoramic views from compartments ensure ultimate relaxation. The luxury of the train is exemplified by its compartments with wood detail and polished brass, three dining cars with French silverware and crystal, and stylish bar car.

Die klassischen Wagen des Venice Simplon aus den 20er und 30er Jahren vermitteln ein Reisegefühl, das an die Romantik und Eleganz dieser Ära erinnert. Sowohl original britische Pullman-Wagons als auch Schlafwagen kommen hier zum Einsatz. Persönliche Stewards und die Panoramafenster der Abteile garantieren ultimative Entspannung. Der Luxus des Zuges spiegelt sich in den Abteilen mit ihren Holzdetails und dem polierten Messing, den drei Speisewagen mit französischem Silber und Kristall sowie dem eleganten Barwagen wider.

Le wagon vintage du Venice Simplon des années 1920 et 1930 offre une réminiscence du romantisme et de l'élégance de cette époque. Deux types de wagons sont utilisés : les originaux British Pullman et les Wagons-Lits. Le personnel de bord et la vue panoramique des compartiments assurent une relaxation optimale. Les compartiments ornés de marqueterie et de cuivre lustré, les trois wagons restaurants équipés d'argenterie et de cristaux ainsi que le bar illustrent tout le luxe de ce train.

Los vagones vintage del Venice Simplon de los años 20 y 30 ofrecen la oportunidad de vivir el romanticismo y elegancia de esa época. En este recorrido se emplean las colecciones originales de los vagones British Pullman y Wagons-Lits. Un azafato personal y vistas panorámicas desde los compartimentos aseguran al pasajero un gran momento de relax. El lujo del tren queda patente en sus compartimentos con detalles de madera y cobre pulido, tres vagones comedor con cubertería francesa de plata y cristal y un elegante vagón-bar.

Le carrozze d'epoca del Venice Simplon, originali restaurati degli anni venti e trenta, rievocano il romanticismo e l'eleganza di quegli anni. Sulla tratta vengono impiegati due tipi di carrozze: le British Pullman e i Wagons-Lits. Steward personali e viste panoramiche dagli scompartimenti assicurano il massimo relax. Il lusso del treno è evidente nel legno lavorato e nell'ottone lucido delle cabine, nella posateria d'argento e nelle cristallerie dei tre vagoni ristorante, nell'elegante carrozza bar.

Passengers aboard the Venice Simplon Orient Express can bask in the elegance in one of the onboard Restaurant Cars (Lalique, Etoile du Nord, and Chinoise) while enjoying the decadent dishes created by French Chefs and ultimate service by Italian waiters.

Wer mit dem Venice Simplon-Orient-Express unterwegs ist, kann in die Eleganz eines der Bord-Restaurants (Lalique, Etoile du Nord und Chinoise) eintauchen und die raffinierten Gerichte der französischen Küchenchefs sowie den ausgezeichneten Service der italienischen Kellner genießen.

Des passagers à bord du Venice Simplon-Orient-Express se détendent dans un des élégants wagons-restaurants (Lalique, Etoile du Nord, et Chinoise) tout en savourant les plats exquis créés par des chefs français et en profitant de l'excellence du service italien.

Los pasajeros a bordo del Venice Simplon Orient-Express pueden deleitarse con la elegancia de los distintos vagones restaurante a bordo (Lalique, Etoile du Nord y Chinoise) mientras disfrutan de los deliciosos platos creados por Chefs franceses y servidos por camareros italianos.

I passeggeri a bordo dell'Orient Express Venice Simplon godono dell'eleganza di una delle Carrozze ristorante (Lalique, Etoile du Nord e Chinoise) mentre gustano piatti decadenti cucinati da chef francesi e serviti da impeccabili camerieri italiani.

CHARACTERISTICS & AMENITIES

Date built	1982
Compartments	12 sleeper cars, 3 dining cars, 1 bar car
Suites	Double Compartment or Cabin Suite for 1 or 2 people
Seats	188
Restaurant capacity	34 – 36 passengers per dining car
Origin	London
Destination	Venice
Itinerary	London – Paris – Buchs – Innsbruck – Verona – Venice
Amenities (Services)	24-hour steward service, international electric sockets, individually-controlled radiators, personal safe

HIRAM BINGHAM

The Hiram Bingham takes passengers on a spectacular journey from Cusco to Machu Picchu offering both luxury and unforgettable landscapes. A guided tour of the highlights takes place upon arrival at the Machu Picchu citadel. The ammenities of the train include two dining cars, observation bar car, and a kitchen car all embracing the elegant and inviting decor of the 1920 Pullman trains.

Der Hiram Bingham bringt seine Passagiere auf einer spektakulären Fahrt von Cusco nach Machu Picchu, wobei er sowohl Luxus als auch unvergessliche Landschaftsausblicke bietet. Zur Reise gehört u. a. eine Führung durch die Ruinenstadt Machu Picchu. Der Zug führt zwei Speisewagen, einen Barwagen mit Panoramafenster und einen Küchenwagen mit sich, die allesamt das elegante und einladende Dekor der Pullmans aus den 20er Jahren aufweisen.

Le Hiram Bingham embarque les passagers à travers un voyage spectaculaire du Cusco au Machu Picchu combinant luxe et paysages inoubliables, l'arrivée à la citadelle du Machu Picchu marquant le point culminant du circuit touristique. Les services du train incluent deux wagons-restaurants, une voiture-bar ainsi qu'une cuisine, l'ensemble dans un élégant et agréable décor caractéristique des trains Pullman des années 1920.

El Hiram Bingham conduce a los pasajeros a través de un viaje espectacular que va desde Cusco hasta Machu Picchu, inmersos en un ambiente lujoso y unos paisajes inolvidables. Al llegar a su destino realizan una visita guiada por los lugares más representativos de la ciudadela de Machu Picchu. Los servicios del tren incluyen dos vagones-restaurante, un vagón-bar y un vagón cocina, todos ellos con la atractiva y elegante decoración de los trenes Pullman de 1920.

L'Hiram Bingham accompagna i passeggeri in uno spettacolare viaggio da Cuzco a Machu Picchu, tra lusso e paesaggi indimenticabili. L'arrivo al complesso monumentale di Machu Picchu è corredato da una visita turistica guidata. Tra i servizi offerti dal treno, due vagoni ristorante, bar panoramico e carrozza cucina, il tutto nell'accogliente eleganza degli arredi delle carrozze Pullman anni venti.

Traveling at a leisurely pace, the Hiram Bingham passes through the changing landscapes starting with the agricultural plains of the Sacred Valley, along the Urubamba river, and approaching the majestic mountains on the way to Machu Picchu.

In gemächlichem Tempo fährt der Hiram Bingham durch wechselnde Landschaften, von den landwirtschaftlich genutzten Flächen des Heiligen Tals, am Urubamba entlang bis zu den herrschaftlichen Gipfeln auf dem Weg nach Machu Picchu.

À vitesse de croisière, le Hiram Bingham traverse un paysage diversifié. Partant des plaines agricoles de la Vallée Sacrée, il longe la rivière Urubamba, s'approchant en chemin des majestueuses montagnes du Machu Picchu.

Viajando en un mar de calma, el Hiram Bingham recorre paisajes muy distintos. Parte de las llanuras agrícolas del Valle Sagrado y sigue el curso del río Urubamba, aproximándose a las majestuosas montañas, en su ruta hacia Machu Picchu.

L'Hiram Bingham attraversa placidamente i paesaggi mutevoli, dalle pianure coltivate della Valle Sacra dove scorre il fiume Urubamba, alle montagne maestose di Machu Picchu.

CHARACTERISTICS & AMENITIES	
Date built	2003
Compartments	2 dining cars, 1 observation/bar car
Suites	only seating – this is a daytime tour train
Seats	84
Restaurant capacity	84
Origin	Cusco
Destination	Machu Picchu
Itinerary	Cusco – Aguas Calientes – Machu Picchu
Amenities (Services)	Day train

BRITISH PULLMAN

Designed with the aura of a "Palace on Wheels" by George Mortimer Pullman, each carriage maintains its original form from the 1920s and 1930s. Carriages are individually named and are unique from one another. Upholding its elegance, carriages are intricately detailed with inlaid mosaic floors, woodwork, and crystal. The deeply upholstered armchairs deliver great comfort while on the journey to its many destinations including UK cities, gardens, castles, and sporting events.

Im Sinne eines „Palastes auf Rädern" von George Mortimer Pullman entworfen, haben die Wagons ihre ursprüngliche Form aus den 20er und 30er Jahren behalten. Jeder Wagen hat einen Namen, keiner ist wie der andere. Allesamt wirken sie mit ihren Mosaikböden und Holz- sowie Kristallarbeiten hochelegant. Die stark gepolsterten Sessel bieten höchsten Komfort, während man sich auf die Reise zu einem der zahlreichen Ziele in britischen Städten, Gärten, Schlössern oder zu Sportveranstaltungen macht.

Conçu tel un « Palace on wheels » par George Mortimer Pullman, chaque wagon a gardé la forme originale des années 1920 et 1930. Les voitures sont individuelles et indépendantes les unes des autres. Maintenant son élégance, chaque wagon est décoré avec minutie par des mosaïques incrustées au sol, une marqueterie et du cristal. Les grands fauteuils offrent un formidable confort durant le voyage et ses divers destinations incluant villes britanniques, jardins, châteaux et événements sportifs.

Diseñado bajo el aura del "Palace on Wheels" de George Mortimer Pullman, los vagones conservan la forma original de los años 20 y 30. Cada compartimiento tiene un nombre y es una pieza única. Los vagones están decorados con intrincados suelos de entarimado de mosaico, ebanistería y cristal. Los viajeros disfrutan del gran comfort que les procuran los mullidos sillones tapizados, mientras viajan a multitud de destinos, que incluyen diversas ciudades del Reino Unido, jardines, castillos y eventos deportivos.

Concepita da George Mortimer Pullman come un "palazzo su ruote", ciascuna carrozza conserva l'aspetto originale degli anni venti e trenta. Ogni vagone ha un proprio nome ed è diverso dagli altri. L'eleganza delle carrozze è ribadita da particolari come i pavimenti a mosaico, il legno lavorato, le cristallerie. Le poltrone imbottite assicurano grande comfort durante il tragitto del treno, tra le cui tappe figurano città, giardini, castelli e avvenimenti sportivi della Gran Bretagna.

A steward preparing carriage Minerva. Complete with the traditional decor of the sovereign British heritage, the British Pullman was designed with the utmost detail. With ultimate service from stewards dressed in elegant uniforms, passengers can make themselves comfortable while surrounded by exquisite Art Deco design.

Ein Steward macht den Waggon Minerva reisefertig. Die Wagen des British Pullman spiegeln mit ihrem detailgetreuen Design das goldene Zeitalter des britischen Empire wider. Durch den ausgezeichneten Service der Stewards in ihren eleganten Uniformen können es sich die Passagiere, umgeben von wunderschönem Art-déco-Design, gut gehen lassen.

Un serveur en train de préparer le wagon Minerva. Dans un décor de pur style anglais, le British Pullman a été conçu jusque dans les moindres détails. Les passagers profitent, grâce à l'excellence du service des stewards vêtus d'un élégant uniforme, d'un voyage agréable entouré d'un somptueux design Art Déco.

Un azafato prepara el compartimiento Minerva. El British Pullman fue diseñado con todo lujo de detalle según la decoración tradicional de herencia soberana británica. Gracias al impecable servicio de los camareros, vestidos con elegantes uniformes, los pasajeros pueden disfrutar de en un gran confort, envueltos por un diseño art deco de lo más exquisito.

Un inserviente prepara il vagone Minerva. Con i suoi arredi ispirati alla migliore tradizione britannica, il British Pullman è stato progettato con una particolare attenzione ai minimi dettagli. I passeggeri sono accolti in ambienti dallo squisito design art déco e assistiti da inservienti in eleganti livree.

CHARACTERISTICS & AMENITIES	
Date built	1920s – 1930s
Compartments	6 parlor cars, 5 dining cars
Suites	Only seating – this is a daytime tour train
Seats	252
Restaurant capacity	20 seats per dining car
Origin	Varied within the United Kingdom
Destination	Varied within the United Kingdom
Itinerary	Varied within the United Kingdom
Amenities (Services)	Day train

ROYAL SCOTSMAN

Upholstered with a plaid that would make a true Scotsman proud, the Royal Scotsman traverses the Scottish countryside on journeys to and from Edinburgh lasting from two to seven nights. One of the most spectacular features of the train is the open-ended observation car, once a 1960 kitchen car and now lovingly converted into a luxury lounge capable of comfortably seating all thirty-two guests. Guests can relax here as the train rides through the heart of the Highlands, past towering mountains and crystal lakes.

Mit einem karierten Stoff bezogen, der jedem Schotten zur Ehre gereichen würde, fährt der Royal Scotsman auf seinen Fahrten von und nach Edinburgh durch die schottische Landschaft. Eine solche Reise dauert zwischen zwei und sieben Übernachtungen. Zu den spektakulärsten Angeboten dieses Zuges gehört der offene Panoramawagen, der in den 60er Jahren einmal als Küchenwagen gedient hatte, heutzutage jedoch liebevoll in eine Luxuslounge verwandelt wurde, in der es sich 32 Gäste bequem machen können. Hier kann man entspannen, während der Zug an Bergen und kristallklaren Seen vorbei das Herz der Highlands durchquert.

Tapissé d'un tissu écossais qui enorgueillerait tout vrai Écossais, le Royal Scotsman traverse la campagne écossaise en partance d'Édimbourg durant deux à sept nuits. Une des caractéristiques les plus spectaculaires du train est l'observatoire situé en fin de wagon. Autrefois, wagon-cuisine dans les années 1960, il a été reconverti avec soin en un bar de luxe capable d'accueillir trente-deux convives. Les voyageurs peuvent se reposer ici lors des passages au cœur des Highlands, ancestrales et majestueuses montagnes et des lacs cristallins.

Con tapizados en telas de cuadrados dignas de orgullo de cualquier escocés que se precie, el Royal Scotsman atraviesa la campiña escocesa con trayectos que tienen su origen y final en Edimburgo y duran de dos a siete noches. Una de la características más destacadas del tren es el observatorio descubierto, situado en la cola del vagón. El que fuera un vagón cocina en los años 60, es hoy día un lujoso lounge capaz de acoger treinta y dos pasajeros cómodamente sentados. Los viajeros pueden relajarse mientras el tren los transporta al corazón de Highlands, recorriendo elevadas montañas y lagos cristalinos.

Ricco di tessuti a scacchi che renderebbero orgoglioso qualsiasi scozzese, il Royal Scotsman propone viaggi, da e per Edimburgo, che possono durare dalle due alle sette notti attraverso i paesaggi naturali della Scozia. Una delle sue caratteristiche più eclatanti è la carrozza panoramica aperta, un ex vagone cucina degli anni sessanta accuratamente trasformato in un raffinato lounge in grado di ospitare con agio tutti e trentadue gli ospiti del treno. Qui i passeggeri possono godersi il proprio relax mentre il Royal Scotsman si inoltra nel cuore delle Highlands, tra imponenti montagne e laghi cristallini.

Interior of a room aboard the Royal Scotsman manifested in true Scottish decor

Innenausstattung eines Abteils des Royal Scotsman in typisch schottischem Stil

Intérieur d'une pièce à bord du Royal Scotsman réalisée en véritable décor écossais

Interior de una habitación a bordo del Royal Scotsman con una decoración de estilo claramente escocés

L'interno, arredato in stile tipicamente scozzese, di una vettura del Royal Scotsman

Observation car where guests can relax and capture some of Scotland's most exquisite sights and landscapes as they go through Perth, Keith, Inverness, Edinburgh, and Boat of Garten.

Während der Zug Perth, Keith, Inverness, Edinburgh und Boat of Garten passiert, können die Gäste im Panorama-Wagen entspannen und einige der schönsten Aussichten auf schottische Landschaften genießen.

Wagon d'observation où les hôtes peuvent se détendre et saisir les plus beaux paysages écossais en passant par Perth, Keith, Inverness, Édimbourg et Boat of Garten.

Vagón observatorio donde los pasajeros pueden relajarse disfrutando de las vistas más espléndidas de Escocia durante el trayecto por Perth, Keith, Inverness, Edimburgo y Boat of Garten.

Gli ospiti possono rilassarsi nella carrozza panoramica e ammirare alcuni dei paesaggi più affascinanti della Scozia mentre attraversano Perth, Keith, Inverness, Edimburgo, e Boat of Garten.

CHARACTERISTICS & AMENITIES	
Date built	1990
Compartments	5 sleeper cars, 2 dining cars, 1 observation car
Suites	16 compartments for 2; 4 compartments for 1
Seats	36
Restaurant capacity	16 – 20 passengers per dining car
Origin	Edinburgh
Destination	Edinburgh
Itinerary	Varied within Scotland
Amenities (Services)	Lower beds, dressing table, wardrobe, individually-controlled heating, ceiling fans, opening windows

EASTERN ORIENT EXPRESS

The Eastern & Oriental Express was the first train to have a route directly from Singapore and Kuala Lumpur to Bangkok. The journey melds the tranquil landscape with the deep historical presence of South East Asia. The environment is reminiscent of "Colonial" ages through the rattan chairs on the verandah, linen suits, and tea dances. With inspiration from Eastern style, the interiors of the carriages are decorated with marquetry.

Der Eastern & Oriental Express war der erste Zug, der auf direkter Strecke von Singapur und Kuala Lumpur nach Bangkok fuhr. Die Reise verbindet friedliche Landschaften und die immer präsente Geschichte Südostasiens. Die Rattanstühle auf der Veranda, die Leinenanzüge und die Teetanzstunden erinnern an frühere Kolonialzeiten. Vom Stil des Ostens inspiriert, sind die Interieurs der Wagen mit Holzintarsien geschmückt.

Le Eastern & Oriental Express fut le premier train direct Singapour – Kuala Lumpur passant par Bangkok. Le voyage combine de tranquilles paysages avec une profonde immersion dans l'histoire du sud-est asiatique. Ses chaises en osier dans la véranda, costumes en lin, ses bals, l'environnement tout entier respire les reminiscences de l'époque coloniale. D'inspiration orientale, les intérieurs des wagons sont décorés de marqueterie.

El Eastern & Oriental Express fue el primer tren que realizó una ruta directa desde Singapur y Kuala Lumpur a Bangkok. En el trayecto se funden un paisaje lleno de calma y la fuerte presencia histórica de sur de Asia. El tren conserva el ambiente del período colonial gracias a las sillas de caña de rattan en la veranda, los trajes de lino y las danzas del té. Inspirado en el estilo del este, el interior de los compartimentos está decorado con marquetería.

L'Eastern & Oriental Express è stato il primo treno a coprire la tratta diretta Singapore – Kuala Lumpur – Bangkok, in un percorso che coniuga i morbidi paesaggi e la storia millenaria del Sud-est asiatico. L'ambientazione rievoca l'epoca coloniale attraverso le sedie in rattan della veranda, le stoffe di lino, i balli organizzati all'ora del tè. Gli interni delle carrozze, di ispirazione orientale, sono abbelliti da intarsi in legno.

top: A Presidential compartment in "day-time" configuration
Die Präsidentensuite während des Tages
Un compartiment présidentiel en configuration « journée »
La *suite* presidencial de día
Una carrozza presidenziale durante il giorno

bottom left: A state compartment
Ein Prachtabteil
Un compartiment d'état
Un compartimento de lujo
Uno scompartimento di Stato

top left: The bar and restaurant possess an Eastern influence in its decor with the use of Chinese and Thai laquer. A Malaysian design is incorporated along with intricately carved walls and engraved mirrors.

In der Bar und im Restaurant kann man in den chinesischen und thailändischen Lackarbeiten einen östlichen Einfluss entdecken. Neben den aufwändig geschnitzten Wänden und gravierten Spiegeln spielt auch ein malayisches Design eine Rolle.

L'usage de la laque chinoise et thaïlandaise dans le bar et le restaurant dénotent une influence orientale. Le design malaisien est également présent sur les murs, abondamment sculptés et les miroirs gravés.

El bar y el restaurante denotan una influencia del Este con el uso de laqueado chino y tailandés en su decoración. El diseño malasio está también presente en las paredes, profusamente talladas y espejos con grabados.

L'arredamento del bar e del ristorante tradisce le influenze orientali nell'uso di mobili laccati cinesi e thailandesi. C'è spazio anche per il gusto malese, presente nelle pareti minuziosamente intagliate e negli specchi incisi.

CHARACTERISTICS & AMENITIES	
Date built	1993
Compartments	2 dining cars and 1 observation car; 18 cars total
Suites	Presidential Suite, State Cabin, Pullman Superior Car (all sleep two)
Seats	132
Restaurant capacity	34 passengers per dining car
Origin	Singapore
Destination	Bangkok
Itinerary	Singapore – Malaysia – Thailand
Amenities (Services)	24-hour steward service, international electric sockets, personal safe, hairdryer, shower en suite

TRANSCANTÁBRICO

The distinctly blue and white Transcantábrico journeys across northern Spain, along the coast. All dinners and lunches are taken at restaurants along the route offering the best of Spanish cuisine and a careful selection of wines. As the only luxury train service in Spain, the Transcantábrico is an opportunity unlike any other and counts among its stops the famed Guggenheim Museum in Bilbao.

Der blau-weiße Transcantábrico fährt an der Küste Nordspaniens entlang. Mittag- und Abendessen werden in Restaurants an der Strecke eingenommen, wo die beste spanische Küche und exquisite Weine serviert werden. Als einzige Luxuszuglinie Spaniens bietet der Transcantábrico einzigartige Möglichkeiten. Zu seinen Haltestellen gehört u. a. das berühmte Guggenheim-Museum in Bilbao.

Le Transcantábrico dans son inimitable combinaison de bleu et blanc voyage à travers l'Espagne du Nord, le long de la côte. Tous les dîners et les déjeuners sont pris le long du trajet dans des restaurants offrant le meilleur de la cuisine espagnole et une excellente sélection de vins. Le Transcantábrico est l'unique train de luxe en Espagne et compte parmi ses arrêts le célèbre Musée Guggenheim de Bilbao.

El inconfundible azul y blanco Transcantábrico recorre la costa del norte de España. Los almuerzos y cenas, y la cuidada selección de vinos que se ofrecen a bordo provienen de algunos de los mejores restaurantes de cocina española, que se encuentran en su ruta. Como uno de los pocos trenes de lujo españoles, el Transcantábrico ofrece la gran oportunidad de visitar el famoso Museo Guggenheim de Bilbao, en una de sus paradas.

L'inconfondibile Transcantábrico bianco e blu effettua il proprio servizio nel Nord della Spagna, principalmente lungo la costa. Pranzi e cene si svolgono in ristoranti disseminati lungo la tratta, dove è possibile gustare il meglio della cucina spagnola e una ricercata selezione di vini. Unico treno di lusso della Spagna, il Transcantábrico propone un'esperienza irripetibile e conta, tra le sue molte tappe, il celebre museo Guggenheim di Bilbao.

The "Green" Spain tour passes through Galicia, Asturias, Cantabria, the Basque Country and Castilla Leon to allow passengers to immerse themselves in the fascinating culture by dining in the best restaurants and experiencing the true beauty of Spanish countryside. Passengers can visit the most remarkable sights when disembarking to reach those most impressive areas that are inaccessible by train.

Die „grüne" Spanientour führt durch Galizien, Asturien, Kantabrien, das Baskenland und Kastilien-León. Der Reisende kann in die faszinierende Kultur des Landes eintauchen, indem er in den besten Restaurants isst und die wahre Schönheit der spanischen Landschaft kennen lernt. Gleichzeitig kann er die herrlichsten Sehenswürdigkeiten besuchen, die allerdings nicht alle vom Zug aus erreichbar sind.

Le Transcantábrico traverse la Galice, les Asturies, la Cantabrie, le Pays Basque et la Castille Léon plongeant les voyageurs dans une culture fascinante grâce aux meilleurs restaurants et à l'authentique beauté de la campagne verte espagnole. Lors des arrêts, les passagers peuvent accéder aux paysages extraordinaires des régions inaccessibles en train.

El Transcantábrico realiza un tour por la España verde. Recorre Galicia, Asturias, Cantabria, el País Vasco y Castilla León, permitiendo a los pasajeros sumergirse en esta fascinante cultura, deleitándose en los mejores restaurantes y acercándose a la verdadera belleza del interior de España. Los pasajeros pueden disfrutar de unas bellas vistas también cuando desembarcan para visitar los lugares más impresionantes, inaccesibles desde el tren.

Toccando la Galizia, le Asturie, la Cantabria, i Paesi Baschi, la Castiglia e León, questo tour "verde" della Spagna settentrionale permette ai passeggeri di immergersi in una cultura affascinante, tra bellezze paesaggistiche e la cucina dei migliori ristoranti locali. I viaggiatori possono inoltre scendere dal treno e visitare luoghi incantevoli non raggiungibili dalla ferrovia.

CHARACTERISTICS & AMENITIES	
Date built	1983
Compartments	26
Suites	For 2 or 3 passengers
Seats	—
Restaurant capacity	All meals are taken at restaurants off the train
Origin	Santiago de Compostela
Destination	León
Itinerary	Santiago de Compostela – Luarca – Gijón – Llanes – Santander – León
Amenities (Services)	Luggage rack, minibar, safe deposit box, wardrobe, writing desk, telephone, hairdryer, air-conditioning, heating

MAJESTIC IMPERATOR

Described as a "palace on rails," the Majestic Imperator is a day train journeying through the centuries-old architecture of exquisite Vienna. In addition to a dinner train complete with red carpet entrance and four-course meal, the Majestic Imperator runs a New Years Express in its lavishly luxurious carriages with a celebration over the river Danube as guests dance the night away.

Der Majestic Imperator wird immer wieder als „Palast auf Schienen" bezeichnet. Er fährt als Tageszug durch die jahrhundertealte Architektur von Wien. Außer einem Speisewagen mit rot ausgelegtem Entrée und Viergängemenü bietet der Majestic Imperator in seinen üppig luxuriösen Wagen einen Sylvesterexpress mit einem Fest über der Donau, auf dem die Gäste die Nacht durchtanzen können.

Décrit comme un « palace sur rails », le Majestic Imperator est un train de jour voyageant à travers le siècle d'or de l'architecture viennoise. En plus du wagon-dîner avec tapis rouge et menu à quatre plats, le Majestic Imperator organise la soirée de nouvel an sur le fleuve Danube dans ses somptueuses voitures de luxe pour que les invités dansent tard dans la nuit.

Apodado como "palacio sobre ruedas", el Majestic Imperator es un tren diurno que recorre la antigua arquitectura de la exquisita ciudad de Viena. El tren da la bienvenida a sus pasajeros con una alfombra roja que los conduce desde el andén a la entrada y después los deleita con un menú de cuatro platos. El Majestic Imperator ofrece la posibilidad de pasar un Fin de Año Express en sus lujosos compartimentos. Los invitados podrán bailar toda la noche en la celebración, que tiene lugar en el río Danubio.

Un "palazzo reale su binari", il Majestic Imperator accompagna i propri passeggeri in un tour delle secolari bellezze architettoniche di Vienna. Oltre a fungere da treno ristorante con tappeto rosso e cena con menù a quattro portate, il Majestic Imperator organizza anche una festa di Capodanno sul Danubio, animando di danze le proprie lussuose carrozze fino al mattino.

top: Salon Elisabeth

left: Candlelight dinner in Excelsior

Dinner bei Kerzenlicht im Excelsior

Dîner aux chandelles à l'Excelsior

Cena a la luz de las velas en el Excelsior

Cena a lume di candela a bordo dell'Excelsior

CHARACTERISTICS & AMENITIES	
Date built	1998
Compartments	6 parlor cars
Suites	Only seating – this is a daytime tour train
Seats	191
Restaurant capacity	149
Origin	Vienna
Destination	Vienna
Itinerary	Vienna
Amenities (Services)	Day train

GRANDLUXE EXPRESS

The GrandLuxe is one of the few luxury trains in the United States, celebrating the style and comfort of the romantic American 1940s and 1950s. The journeys of the GrandLuxe cover the United States from coast to coast and even into the Copper Canyon of Mexico. The fully restored vintage coaches—one complete with a piano—navigate the majestic countryside and guests have the opportunity to relax in numerous lounge, bar, or domed observation carriages as the landscape glides by.

Der GrandLuxe ist einer der wenigen Luxuszüge der USA, der den Stil und die Bequemlichkeit der romantischen 40er und 50er Jahre in den Staaten feiert. Die Reisen des GrandLuxe führen durch ganz Nordamerika von Küste zu Küste und sogar bis in den mexikanischen Copper Canyon. Die gänzlich aufgearbeiteten alten Wagons – einer mit Klavier – passieren die majestätische Landschaft, während sich die Gäste in den zahlreichen Lounge- und Barwagen oder dem Panoramawagen mit Kuppeldach entspannen können.

Le GrandLuxe est un des seuls trains de luxe aux États-Unis, hommage au style et au confort du romantisme américain des années 1940 et 1950. Le parcours du GrandLuxe couvre toute la côte américaine jusqu'au Copper Canyon de Mexico. Les wagons vintage entièrement restaurés dont un avec piano naviguent à travers une campagne majestueuse. Les passagers peuvent se détendre dans les nombreux lounges, bar ou dans les coupoles des compartiments d'observation d'où voir défiler le payasage.

El GrandLuxe es uno de los pocos trenes de lujo en Estados Unidos que rememoran el estilo y confort de los románticos años 40 y 50 americanos. El viaje del GrandLuxe cubre los Estados Unidos de costa a costa hasta el Cañon Copper de México. Los vagones vintage –uno de ellos con piano incluido– totalmente restaurados navegan a través de los majestuosos campos y los pasajeros tienen la oportunidad de relajarse en los numerosos lounge, bares o en las cúpulas de los compartimentos observatorio a medida que cambia el paisaje tras la ventana.

Il GrandLuxe è fra i pochi treni di lusso degli Stati Uniti, omaggio allo stile e al comfort dei romantici anni quaranta e cinquanta americani. Il treno attraversa il paese da una costa all'altra, spingendosi fino alla Barranca del Cobre in Messico. Le carrozze d'epoca completamente restaurate, di cui una provvista di pianoforte, esplorano paesaggi maestosi mentre gli ospiti approfittano delle opportunità di relax offerte dai vari bar e lounge o ammirano gli scorci mozzafiato dalle carrozze panoramiche a cupola.

Traveling along landscapes that can only be experienced by rail to bring passengers closer to nature.

Eine Reise durch Landschaften, die man nur mit dem Zug erreichen kann. Hier kommen die Passagiere der Natur näher.

En roulant à travers les paysages, seul le train offre l'expérience de plonger les passagers dans la nature.

Este tren permite viajar por paisajes inaccesibles de otro modo para el viajero, y le acerca a la naturaleza.

Viaggiare attraverso paesaggi godibili solo in treno favorisce il contatto con la natura.

CHARACTERISTICS & AMENITIES	
Date built	1948 – 1958
Compartments	Sleeper cars, dining cars, dome car, observation car
Suites	Gold Suite, Grand Suite, Classic Presidential Suite, Parlor Suite, Vintage Pullman, Triple Suite, Single Sleeper Grand Class, Single Sleeper
Seats	—
Restaurant capacity	88 passengers per dining car
Origin	Varied within North America
Destination	Varied within North America
Itinerary	Varied within North America
Amenities (Services)	En suite bathroom, lectures on-board, explorations off-board, guided tours, overnight hotel stays

BLUE TRAIN

The Blue Train boasts presidents and kings in the long list of distinguished guests it has transported between Pretoria and Cape Town aboard one of the most luxurious trains in the world. The menus feature a selection of local cuisine from Karoo lamb to Knysna oysters accompanied by award-winning cultivars from the Cape winelands, all serving as the perfect complement to the amazing views. The Blue Train navigates smoothly through the landscapes of South Africa with the beauty outside the train only paralleled by the beauty inside.

Zur langen Liste der distinguierten Gäste des Blue Train, einem der luxuriösesten Züge der Welt, gehören Staatspräsidenten und Könige, die schon auf seiner Fahrt zwischen Pretoria und Kapstadt an Bord waren. Auf der Speisekarte finden sich lokale Spezialitäten wie Karoo-Lamm oder Knysna-Austern sowie ausgezeichnete Weine aus der Kap-Region, die perfekt zu dem atemberaubenden Ausblick aus dem Zug passen. Der Blue Train gleitet sanft durch die Landschaft Südafrikas, wobei die Schönheit außerhalb des Zuges nur von der Schönheit im Zug erreicht wird.

Le Blue Train peut se vanter de compter présidents et rois parmi sa longue liste d'invités distingués transportés entre Pretoria et Cape Town, à bord d'un des trains les plus luxueux au monde. Ses menus offrent une sélection des meilleurs plats de la cuisine locale tel que l'agneau à la Karoo ou les huîtres de Knysna, accompagnés par un des vins primés des vignes de Cape Town, le tout sur fond de vues imprenables. Le Blue Train navigue doucement à travers les paysages de l'Afrique du Sud dont la beauté égale celle de la décoration intérieure.

El Blue Train, uno de los trenes más lujosos del mundo, puede alardear de haber transportado de Pretoria a Ciudad del Cabo a una larga lista de distinguidos clientes, entre los que se cuentan presidentes y reyes. Sus menús ofrecen una selección de la mejor cocina local como el filete de cordero a la Karoo y las ostras de Knysna, acompañado por uno de los galardonados vinos de los viñedos de Cabo, y todo ello servido como complemento a unas espectaculares vistas. El tren se desliza suavemente a través de los paisajes de Sudáfrica desvelando a los pasajeros una belleza exterior solo comparable a la del interior.

Fra i treni più lussuosi al mondo, il Blue Train può vantare un lungo elenco di passeggeri illustri, tra cui anche re e capi di stato, che hanno viaggiato sulla tratta Pretoria – Città del Capo. I menù prevedono una selezione di piatti locali che vanno dall'agnello del Karoo alle ostriche di Knysna, accompagnati da vini prodotti con i vitigni sudafricani più pregiati, il tutto a perfetto complemento degli spettacolari panorami. Il treno attraversa sinuoso i paesaggi sudafricani, la cui bellezza trova un degno corrispettivo in quella degli interni.

Luxury carriages maintain a classic elegance from its creation in 1923.

Die Luxuswagen haben ihre klassische Eleganz seit ihrer Erbauung im Jahr 1923 bewahrt.

Les wagons de luxe gardent leur élégance classique de leur création en 1923.

Los lujosos vagones destacan por su elegancia clásica desde que se crearon en 1923.

Le carrozze di lusso mantengono la loro classica eleganza fin dalla loro costruzione nel 1923.

CHARACTERISTICS & AMENITIES	
Date built	1997 – 1998
Compartments	2/3 sleeping cars, 1 dining car, 2 lounge cars
Suites	29/37 suites for two
Seats	58/74
Restaurant capacity	42
Origin	Pretoria
Destination	Cape Town
Itinerary	Pretoria – Kimberly – Cape Town
Amenities (Services)	Down duvets, phones, en suite bathroom, wardrobe, writing desk, entertainment center, air conditioning

ROVOS RAIL

With refurnished and wood-panelled coaches and five-star luxury cuisine, Rovos Rail transports passengers into a lost era elegance and romance as it transports them through the countryside of South Africa. In addition to its service within South Africa, in 2010 Rovos Rail will open an unprecedented luxury route from Cape Town to Cairo, Egypt, covering the whole of Africa by rail and air in the lavish style to which passengers are accustomed to.

Rovos Rail mit seinen restaurierten, holzverkleideten Wagons und Fünf-Sterne-Küche führt auf seiner Fahrt durch Südafrika seine Gäste in eine vergangene Epoche der Eleganz und Romantik. Außer in Südafrika wird Rovos Rail ab 2010 auch eine bisher unerschlossene Luxusroute von Kapstadt nach Kairo in Ägypten eröffnen und somit ganz Afrika auf Schienen und in der Luft erschließen und das in dem verschwenderischen Stil, an den seine Passagiere gewöhnt sind.

Ses wagons réaménagés et en lambris, son restaurant de luxe cinq étoiles, le Rovos Rail évoque une élégance, une romance aujourd'hui perdue, transportant ses passagers à travers la campagne de l'Afrique du Sud. D'autre part, le Rovos Rail ouvrira en 2010 une ligne exclusive de luxe de Cape Town au Caire couvrant ainsi toute l'Afrique par terre et air toujours dans ce style extravagant qui lui est propre.

Con vagones reformados y totalmente revestidos de madera y una cocina de cinco estrellas, el Rovos Rail transporta a sus pasajeros a una época lejana de elegancia y romanticismo mientras recorren el interior de Sudáfrica. Además de su servicio ferroviario en Sudáfrica, a partir de 2010 Rovos Rail abrirá una nueva ruta desde Ciudad del Cabo hasta El Cairo, Egipto, y cubrirá todo el territorio africano por aire y por tierra con este tren de gran estilo.

Con le sue carrozze rimodernate e rivestite in legno e la sua cucina cinque stelle, la Rovos Rail proietta i passeggeri nell'eleganza e nel romanticismo di tempi perduti, mentre le sue carrozze attraversano i paesaggi naturali del Sudafrica. In aggiunta ai servizi in territorio nazionale, nel 2010 la Rovos Rail inaugurerà una linea di lusso senza precedenti che coprirà, fra tragitti aerei e ferroviari, l'intera lunghezza del continente africano, da Città del Capo al Cairo, nello sfarzo che da sempre contraddistingue la compagnia.

1924 Dining car "Shangani"

Der „Shangani"-Speisewagen von 1924

Voiture restaurant « Shangani » de 1924

1924 Coche restaurante "Shangani"

La carrozza ristorante "Shangani" è del 1924

CHARACTERISTICS & AMENITIES	
Date built	1989
Compartments	Sleeper cars, 2 dining cars, 1 observation car, 1 lounge car
Suites	Pullman Suite, Deluxe Royal Suite
Seats	42/72
Restaurant capacity	42 passengers per dining car
Origin	Pretoria
Destination	Cape Town
Itinerary	Pretoria – Kimberly – Majiesfontein – Cape Town
Amenities (Services)	Air conditioning, twin or double bed, bar fridge, 24-hour steward service, en suite bathroom, hairdryer

VICTORIA EXPRESS

With the renovation of a pair of Pullman cars and the addition of a restaurant car, the Victoria Express began its luxury sleeper service bringing Victoria Sapa Hotel guests from Hanoi to Lao Cai. The service runs six days a week as part of a regular overnight service and is only available to hotel guests because of its popularity. The dining experience aboard the Victoria Express offers a freshly prepared four-course meal by French-trained chef, Alain Nguyen and magnificent landscapes as the train travels North Vietnam.

Der Victoria Express begann seinen Luxusschlafwagenservice mit der Instandsetzung zweier Pullman-Wagons und eines zusätzlichen Speisewagens. Nun können die Gäste des Victoria Sapa Hotels damit von Hanoi nach Lao Cai reisen. Der Zug fährt sechs Mal die Woche als Teil eines regulären Nachtzugs und steht aufgrund seiner Beliebtheit nur den Hotelgästen zur Verfügung. Im Speisewagen kann man frisch zubereitete Vier-Gänge-Menüs von dem in Frankreich ausgebildeten Chefkoch Alain Nguyen zu sich nehmen, während man die wunderbare Landschaft Nordvietnams genießt.

Avec la rénovation de deux voitures Pullman et de l'adjonction d'un wagon-restaurant, le Victoria Express a initié son service de train de nuit de luxe portant les clients de l'Hôtel Victoria Sapa d'Hanoi à Lao Cai. En raison de son immense popularité, le service de nuit six jours par semaine n'est disponible que pour les hôtes de l'hôtel. Son restaurant offre un menu à quatre plats préparé sur place par le chef cuisinier de formation française Alain Nguyen ainsi que de splendides paysages à travers le nord du Vietnam.

El Victoria Express comenzó a ofrecer su coche-cama de lujo como servicio para los huéspedes del Hotel Victoria Sapa, que se trasladaban desde Hanoi hasta Lao Cai, en un par de vagones Pullman renovados, con un vagón restaurante adicional. El tren realiza este trayecto nocturno seis días a la semana. Debido a su gran popularidad, este servicio está exclusivamente reservado a los invitados del hotel. A bordo del Victoria Express los viajeros disfrutan de una comida de cuatro platos preparados por un Chef con formación francesa, Alain Nguyen, mientras el tren recorre los magníficos paisajes, camino al Norte de Vietnam.

Restaurate due carrozze Pullman e aggiunto un vagone ristorante, il Victoria Express ha inaugurato il proprio servizio notturno di lusso con il trasferimento da Hanoi a Lao Cai degli ospiti dell'hotel Victoria Sapa. Il trasporto si svolge in nottata e il servizio è attivo sei giorni alla settimana ma riservato, a causa del suo enorme successo, agli ospiti dell'albergo. Il Victoria Express offre una cena con menù a quattro portate proposta da Alain Nguyen, chef locale di formazione francese, e la possibilità di ammirare gli splendidi paesaggi nordvietnamiti attraversati dal treno.

left: Le Tonkin dining carriage

Der Speisewagen Le Tonkin

Voiture restaurant Le Tonkin

El coche restaurante Le Tonkin

Carrozza ristorante Le Tonkin

CHARACTERISTICS & AMENITIES	
Date built	2000
Compartments	2 sleeper cars, 1 dining car
Suites	10 cabins (4 beds each); 4 cabins (2 beds each)
Seats	48
Restaurant capacity	44
Origin	Hanoi
Destination	Lao Cai
Itinerary	Hanoi – Lao Cai
Amenities (Services)	Four-course meal prepared on-board

ROYAL CANADIAN PACIFIC

European royalty, Prime Ministres, and an array of Hollywood celebrities have journeyed along the Canadian Rockies to experience the traditional elegance, gourmet cuisine, and fine wines aboard the Royal Canadian Pacific. With fully restored vintage Canadian Pacific business cars built between 1916 and 1931, the Royal Canadian Pacific launched its service in 2002. Guests can participate in public excursions such as fly-fishing in the pristine Canadian lakes, golfing on various championship courses, and a Canadian Rockies experience that illustrates the rich Canadian heritage.

Mitglieder europäischer Königshäuser, Premierminister und eine große Anzahl Hollywoodstars sind schon entlang der kanadischen Rocky Mountains gefahren, um die traditionelle Eleganz, die Gourmetküche und die erlesenen Weine an Bord des Royal Canadian Pacific zu genießen. Die Bahngesellschaft ließ die Wagons der Canadian Pacific, die zwischen 1916 und 1931 erbaut wurden, restaurieren und brachte sie 2002 wieder in Betrieb. Die Gäste können an Ausflügen teilnehmen und so das reiche kanadische Kulturerbe erleben – wie z. B. beim Fliegenfischen an den glasklaren kanadischen Seen, beim Golfen auf verschiedenen Championship-Kursen oder in den kanadischen Rockies.

Premiers ministres, cour européenne ainsi qu'un grand nombre de célébrités d'Hollywood ont voyagé le long des Canadien Rockies pour connaître l'élégance traditionnelle, la cuisine de gourmet et les vins fins à bord du Royal Canadian Pacific. Le service du Royal Canadian Pacific a été ouvert en 2002 avec la restauration des wagons d'affaires Canadian Pacific construits entre 1916 et 1931. Les invités peuvent participer aux excursions comme la pêche à la mouche dans les lacs canadiens, jouer au golf dans les divers championnats et une expérience à travers les Canadien Rockies illustrant toute la richesse du Canada.

A bordo del Royal Canadian Pacific han viajado miembros de la realeza europea, primeros ministros y un gran número de estrellas y personalidades holliwoodienses, que han aprovechado la ocasión de recorrer las Montañas Rocosas de Canadá inmersos en un ambiente de elegancia clásica, y saboreando cocina gourmet y vinos selectos. En 2002 Royal Canadian Pacific inauguró el servicio business, en los vagones vintage, que fueron construidos entre 1916 y 1931 y han sido totalmente restaurados. Los pasajeros pueden participar en excursiones públicas como la pesca con mosca en los prístinos lagos de Canadá, o los campeonatos de golf, y disfrutar de la belleza de las Montañas Rocosas, una muestra de la riqueza del patrimonio natural canadiense.

Aristocratici europei, primi ministri e uno stuolo di celebrità hollywoodiane hanno attraversato le Montagne Rocciose Canadesi potendo godere della tradizionale eleganza, della cucina da gourmet e dei vini prestigiosi offerti dalla Royal Canadian Pacific. La compagnia ha inaugurato il proprio servizio nel 2002, utilizzando carrozze business della Canadian Pacific risalenti agli anni 1916 – 1931 e completamente restaurate. Gli ospiti possono prendere parte a un ventaglio di attività aperte al pubblico, dalla pesca con la mosca negli immacolati laghi canadesi al golf su percorsi professionistici, fino alle escursioni sulle Montagne Rocciose Canadesi grazie alle quali potranno toccare con mano la ricchezza del patrimonio culturale locale.

Storm Mountain lookout, Alberta

Blick auf den Storm Mountain in Alberta/Kanada

Point de vue sur Storm Mountain à Alberta

Vista a la montaña Storm, Alberta, Canadá

Vista sulla Storm Mountain, Alberta

left: Bridge at Lundbreck Falls

Brücke über die Lundbreck Falls

Le pont à Lundbreck Falls

Puente sobre las cataratas Lundbreck

Ponte sulle Lundbreck Falls

The menu in the Craigellachie dining car includes a variety of traditional and exotic dishes from both land and sea.

Auf der Speisekarte des Craigellachie-Speisewagens findet sich eine Auswahl an traditionellen und exotischen Gerichten von Land und Meer.

Le menu du wagon-restaurant Craigellachie inclut une variété de plats traditionnels et exotiques des régions intérieures et côtières.

El menú en el vagón comedor Craigellachie propone una gran variedad de platos tradicionales y exóticos de mar y tierra.

Il menù della carrozza ristorante Craigellachie comprende un ampio assortimento di piatti tradizionali ed esotici, tanto di pesce quanto di carne.

CHARACTERISTICS & AMENITIES	
Date built	2000 (Original cars were built in 1916 – 1931)
Compartments	2 sleeper cars, 1 lounge car, 1 dining car, 5 business cars
Suites	13 cabins for two; 6 cabins for 1
Seats	32
Restaurant capacity	32 passengers per dining car
Origin	Calgary
Destination	Calgary
Itinerary	Varied within Canada and the Canadian Rockies
Amenities (Services)	Closet, luggage storage, personal safe, hairdryer, robe

GOLDEN CHARIOT

With Bangalore to both begin and end its luxurious journey through the landscapes and past of India, the Golden Chariot takes its passengers to sites of centuries-old architecture and to glorious golden beaches. The interiors of the train are inspired by the aesthetics of Halebid and Hampi, some of India's oldest cities, and this history is melded seamlessly with the modern as it incorporates technology and business into the journey, providing additional coaches for conference rooms and fitness centres.

Mit Bangalore als Ausgangs- und Endpunkt fährt der Golden Chariot durch die Landschaften und die Vergangenheit Indiens. Seine Passagiere besuchen Jahrhunderte alte Bauten und fantastische goldene Strände. Das Innere des Zuges wurde von der Ästhetik von Halebid und Hampi inspiriert, zwei der ältesten Städte Indiens. Geschichte verbindet sich hier nahtlos mit der Moderne, denn in den Zug fließen Technologie und Business mit ein. So gibt es Extrawagen mit Konferenzräumen und Fitnessstudios.

Au départ et à l'arrivée de Bangalore, dans un voyage de luxe à travers les paysages et le passé de l'Inde, le Golden Chariot emmène ses passagers dans les siècles d'histoire de l'architecture indienne et les plus célèbres plages. L'intérieur du train est inspiré par l'esthétique de Halebid et Hampi, parmi les plus vieilles villes de l'Inde et se mélange à la modernité avec l'incorporation de technologies de pointe et des wagons supplémentaires pour les salles de réunions et d'entraînement de fitness.

Bangalore es la ciudad de origen y destino de un lujoso viaje a través de los paisajes e historia de India. El Golden Chariot transporta a sus pasajeros a gloriosas playas doradas y a lugares cuya arquitectura se remonta a varios siglos de antigüedad. Los interiores del tren se han inspirado en la estética de Halebid y Hampi, dos de las ciudades más antiguas de India. Historia y modernidad se funden en este tren, ya que incorpora nuevas tecnologías y servicios para el mundo empresarial como vagones equipados con salas de conferencias. El Golden Chariot dispone también de centros de fitness.

Partendo e arrivando a Bengalore, il Golden Chariot conduce i propri passeggeri alla scoperta dei paesaggi naturali e della storia dell'India, in un raffinato viaggio che tocca centenari siti architettonici e spiagge dorate. Gli interni del treno si ispirano all'arte di Halebid e Hampi, due tra le più antiche città indiane, ma sul Golden Chariot questo prezioso patrimonio storico va a braccetto con la modernità delle tecnologie e del business, come dimostrano le carrozze adibite a sala conferenze e centro fitness.

left: Nala dining car

Der Nala-Speisewagen

Voiture restaurant Nala

El coche restaurant Nala

Carrozza ristorante Nala

top right: Ayurveda center with spa and gym

Ayurveda-Raum mit Wellness- und Fitness-Center

Centre Ayurveda avec spa et salle de gymnastique

Centro de Ayurveda con zona Spa y gimnasio

centro Ayurveda con spazio wellness e fitness

middle: Furniture inspired by Mysore and Hoysala architecture

Mobiliar inspiriert durch die Architektur von Mysore und Hoysala

Ameublement inspiré par l'architecture de Mysore et Hoysala

Muebles inspirados en la arquitectura de Mysore y Hoysala

Arredi ispirati all'architettura di Mysore e Hoysala

bottom: Sleeping chamber

Schlafwagen

chambre à coucher

Coche cama

Camera da letto

Madira Lounge Bar

CHARACTERISTICS & AMENITIES	
Date built	2007
Compartments	11 passenger cars, 1 lounge/bar car, 2 dining cars, 1 gym car, 1 conference car
Suites	44 cabins for two
Seats	88
Restaurant capacity	2 restaurants
Origin	Bangalore
Destination	Bangalore
Itinerary	Bangalore – Srirangapatnam – Mysore – Kabini – Shravanabelagola – Belur – Halebid – Hampi – Badami – Aihole – Pattadakal – Goa
Amenities (Services)	Air conditioning, writing desk

GOLDEN EAGLE

With modern amenities from underfloor heating and LCD screens in each suite, the Golden Eagle augments the traditional splendor of a rail journey across Russia on the Trans-Siberian Express. The two elegantly designed restaurant cars offer chef-prepared dishes using the freshest local ingredients such as borscht and omul, a fish from Lake Baikal.

Mit modernen Annehmlichkeiten wie Fußbodenheizung und LCD-Bildschirmen in jeder Suite übertrifft der Golden Eagle die Pracht einer traditionellen transsibirischen Eisenbahnfahrt durch Russland. Die zwei eleganten Speisewagen bieten Gerichte vom Chefkoch, zubereitet mit den frischesten lokalen Zutaten, wie Borschtsch oder Omul, einem Fisch aus dem Baikalsee.

Grâce à de modernes aménagements comme un chauffage au sol et des écrans LCD dans chaque suite, le Golden Eagle exalte la splendeur traditionnelle du voyage dans l'Express Trans-sibérien à travers la Russie. Les deux wagons-restaurant élégamment conçus offrent des plats, préparés à base d'ingrédients locaux frais, tel que le bortsch et le omul, un poisson du Lac Baikal.

El Golden Eagle otorga un mayor esplendor al tradicional trayecto a través de Rusia a bordo del Trans-Siberian Express, ofreciendo nuevas prestaciones, como calefacción por suelo radiante y pantallas LCD en cada suite. Dos elegantes vagones restaurante ofrecen una selección de platos elaborados por los chefs con los ingredientes más frescos como el borscht y omul, un pescado del lago Baikal.

Le tecnologie all'avanguardia del Golden Eagle, dal sistema di riscaldamento a pannelli radianti agli schermi LCD collocati in tutte le suite, aggiungono nuovi motivi al fascino tradizionale di un viaggio in treno attraverso la Russia a bordo del Trans-Siberian Express. Nelle due eleganti carrozze ristorante è possibile gustare un borsch o altri piatti squisiti preparati con gli ingredienti locali più freschi, come l'omul, un pesce pescato nel lago Bajkal.

page 88/89: The bar car is a place to socialize and relax. It is open until the last person leaves.

Im Barwagen kann man unter Leute kommen und sich entspannen. Er bleibt offen, bis der letzte Gast gegangen ist.

Le wagon-bar est un endroit de détente et de rencontre. Il reste ouvert jusqu'à ce que les derniers partent.

El vagón bar es un lugar para entablar relaciones sociales y relajarse. Permanece abierto hasta que lo abandona el último pasajero.

Luogo ideale per gli incontri e il relax, la carrozza bar resta aperta finché l'ultimo ospite gradisce rimanere.

CHARACTERISTICS & AMENITIES	
Date built	2007
Compartments	12 sleeping cars, 2 dining cars, 1 bar car
Suites	Gold Cabins and Silver Cabins
Seats	120
Restaurant capacity	64 passengers per dining car
Origin	Moscow
Destination	Vladivostok
Itinerary	Moscow – Kazan –Yekaterinburg – Novosibirsk – Irkutsk – Ulan Ude – Ulan Baatar –Vladivostok
Amenities (Services)	Power showers, underfloor heating, DVD-CD player, air conditioning, en suite bathrooms

DECCAN ODYSSEY

The Deccan Odyssey is one of the most luxurious ways to traverse through the heart of India. Passengers visit the beautiful beaches of Goa and the historic Ajanta caves and along the way are treated to a massage center, spa, and steam bath—all aboard the train itself. The journey through the legendary land spans a full week, allowing guests onboard the opportunity to enjoy both the beauty outside the train and the service and splendor within.

Mit dem Deccan Odyssey reist man auf luxuriöseste Weise durch das Herz Indiens. Die Passagiere besuchen die herrlichen Strände von Goa oder die historischen Ajanta-Höhlen und können sich an Bord des Zuges in einem Massage- und Wellnesscenter oder bei einem Dampfbad entspannen. Die Reise durch das sagenhafte Land dauert eine Woche, so dass man genügend Zeit hat, sowohl die Schönheit vor den Zugfenstern als auch den Luxus im Zuginneren zu genießen.

Le Deccan Odyssey est une des façons les plus luxueuses de traverser le cœur de l'Inde. Des arrêts sont prévus sur les plus belles plages de Goa ainsi qu'une visite des grottes historiques d'Ajanta. Au long du voyage sont proposés massages, spas et hammam à bord du train même. Le voyage sur cette terre légendaire s'étend sur une semaine complète, permettant ainsi aux invités de jouir tant de la beauté à l'extérieur du train que du service et du luxe à l'intérieur.

Viajar a bordo del Deccan Odyssey es una de las maneras más lujosas de atravesar el corazón de India. Los pasajeros visitan las bonitas playas de Goa y las históricas cuevas de Ajanta, y en el trayecto disfrutan del spa, los baños de vapor y reciben tratamientos en el centro de masajes a bordo. Una semana de viaje a través de esta tierra legendaria permite a los pasajeros deleitarse con la belleza exterior y con los servicios y el esplendor que ofrece este tren.

Il Deccan Odyssey rappresenta uno dei modi più lussuosi di attraversare il cuore dell'India. I passeggeri visitano le splendide spiagge di Goa e le storiche grotte di Ajanta coccolandosi, lungo tutto il viaggio, nel centro massaggi, nella spa e nel bagno turco in funzione a bordo del treno: una settimana di viaggio in una terra leggendaria che offre agli ospiti l'opportunità di godere tanto delle bellezze naturali all'esterno del treno, quanto dell'eleganza e del servizio al suo interno.

CHARACTERISTICS & AMENITIES	
Date built	2004
Compartments	13 sleeper cars, 2 restaurant cars, 1 conference car, 1 spa car, 1 lounge/bar car
Suites	Regular Suites and Presidential Suites
Seats	92
Restaurant capacity	36 per dining car
Origin	Mumbai
Destination	Mumbai
Itinerary	Mumbai – Jigadh – Tarkali – Goa – Pune – Aurangabad – Ajanta – Mumbai
Amenities (Services)	Conference room, library, bar, massage center, spa, steam bath, gym, beauty parlor, business center, mini pantry, phone, television

MODERN
TRAINS

MODERN TRAINS

Today, modern trains continue to be faster, safer and offer a higher level of comfort and greater benefits. More than just trips for enjoyment, they have also become an option that is valued more and more by executives and business professionals. On one hand, train travel acts as a time saver when compared to other means of transportation as it drives passangers to the city center and it provides an added window of time that allows them to continue working while onboard—including holding meetings in comfortable rooms. However, we also know that it gives the option to travel to different places with all the commodities and services made possible by the latest leading technology.

Heutzutage sind moderne Züge schneller und sicherer denn je. Sie bieten mehr Komfort und Bequemlichkeiten und offerieren nicht nur Vergnügungsreisen, sondern haben sich auch für Führungskräfte und Geschäftsleute zu einer echten Option gewandelt. Zum einen kann man mit der Bahn im Gegensatz zu anderen Verkehrsmitteln Zeit sparen, da der Reisende direkt ins Zentrum der Städte gebracht wird und man die Stunden an Bord zum Arbeiten nutzen und sogar Meetings abhalten kann. Zum anderen vermag man zu verschiedenen Orten zu gelangen und das mit all den Annehmlichkeiten und dem Service, den neue Technologien ermöglichen.

Chaque fois plus rapides, plus sûrs, les trains modernes offrent un haut niveau de confort et de plus grandes prestations. En dehors des voyages touristiques, ces trains sont également une option aujourd'hui de plus en plus choisie par les hommes d'affaires. D'une part, ils représentent une économie de temps par rapport à d'autres moyens de transport, puisqu'ils conduisent jusque dans les centres des villes, d'autre part, ils offrent l'avantage de permettre de travailler à bord ou de donner des réunions dans des salles adaptées à cet effet. Y seront également présentés des trains exclusivement touristiques voyageant dans différentes parties de la planète, offrant tout le confort et les services d'une technologie de pointe.

Son cada vez más rápidos, más seguros y ofrecen un nivel más alto de confort y mayores prestaciones. Más allá de los viajes de placer también son una opción cada vez más valorada por parte de los ejecutivos. Por un lado, representa un ahorro de tiempo respecto a otros medios de transporte, ya que conduce al mismo centro de la ciudad, además tienen la ventaja añadida de que permiten seguir trabajando a bordo —incluso celebrar reuniones en cómodas salas—. También conoceremos otras opciones para hacer turismo por otros rincones, con todas las comodidades y servicios que facilita la tecnología más puntera.

I treni moderni sono sempre più veloci e sicuri, in grado di offrire prestazioni maggiori e un più elevato livello di comfort. Oltre che per i viaggi di piacere, costituiscono oggi un'alternativa sempre più allettante per professionisti e uomini d'affari: il treno, infatti, arrivando fino al cuore della città, permette notevoli risparmi di tempo rispetto ad altri mezzi di trasporto ma offre anche la possibilità di lavorare a bordo od organizzare riunioni in un ambiente confortevole. Per non parlare dell'opportunità di raggiungere le mete turistiche più disparate potendo usufruire delle comodità e dei servizi resi possibili dalle moderne tecnologie.

AVE

TGV EST EUROPÉEN

On June 10, 2007, a new line, the TGV Est Européen, opened linking Paris to 23 destinations in Eastern France and 10 international destinations. The TGV set French record when it peaked at 200 mph on a test run. The new TGV running on the TGV Est Européen line travels at a speed 12 mph faster than the other TGV routes, offers 3 inches more leg room, and a more modern design by Christian Lacroix.

Am 10. Juni 2007 wurde eine neue Linie, der TGV Est Européen, eröffnet, um Paris mit 23 Reisezielen in Ostfrankreich und 10 internationalen Städten zu verbinden. Der TGV stellte einen französischen Rekord auf, als er mit 320 km/h die Testfahrt bestand. Der neue TGV fährt auf der TGV Est Européen-Linie mit einer 19 km/h schnelleren Geschwindigkeit als die anderen TGV, bietet circa 7 cm mehr Raum für die Beine und ein moderneres Design von Christian Lacroix.

Le 10 juin 2007, une nouvelle ligne, le TGV Est Européen, ouvre à Paris desservant 23 destination dans l'est de la France et 10 à niveau international. Ces rames circulent à 320 km/h, soit 20 km/h au dessus de la vitesse pratiquée sur les autres axes TGV et offrent toutes 7 cm supplémentaires entres les sièges et un design moderne grâce aux nouveaux intérieurs dessinés par Christian Lacroix.

El 10 de junio de 2007, el TGV Est Euopéen abrió su conexión entre París y 23 destinos en el Este de Francia y otros 10 internacionales. El TGV batió su récord de máxima velocidad los 320 km/h durante un ejercicio de prueba. El nuevo TGV que circula en la línea del TGV Est Européen viaja a una velocidad que supera en 20 km/h a los TGV de otras rutas, ofrece 7 cm más de espacio entre los asientos y un moderno diseño de Christian Lacroix.

Il 10 giugno 2007 è stata aperta al pubblico una nuova linea, la LGV Est européenne, che collega Parigi a 23 località della Francia orientale e 10 destinazioni internazionali. Durante un viaggio di collaudo, questo TGV aveva stabilito il nuovo record mondiale di velocità sfiorano i 320 km/h. Il nuovo TGV che effettua servizio sulla TGV Est viaggia a una velocità di circa 20 km/h superiore rispetto alle altre tratte ad alta velocità, offre quasi 7 cm di spazio in più per le gambe dei passeggeri e un design più moderno firmato Christian Lacroix.

The TGV Est Européen is the first high-speed line to run through France since 2007 traveling at speeds up to 200 mph.

Dieser TGV ist der erste Hochgeschwindigkeitszug, der seit 2007 Frankreich durchquert und zwar mit einer Geschwindigkeit von bis zu 320 km/h.

Le TGV Est Européen est, depuis 2007, le premier train à grande vitesse traversant la France roulant à une vitesse de 320 km/h.

En 2007, el TGV Est Européen se convirtió en el primer tren de alta velocidad que atravesó Francia a una velocidad de 320 km/h.

Il TGV Est Européen è il primo treno ad alta velocità a viaggiare in territorio francese, a partire dal 2007, a una velocità di 320 km/h.

Second class cabin detailed with stylized passenger armchairs and chat bars designed to create an atmostphere similar to a lounge of a boutique hotel.

Ein Abteil zweiter Klasse mit stylischen Sitzen und Chatbars, dazu entworfen, eine Atmosphäre wie in der Lobby eines Boutique-Hotels entstehen zu lassen.

Détail des cabines de seconde classe avec ses elegants sièges et des chat-bars conçus pour créer une atmosphère similaire à celle d'un salon d'un hôtel boutique.

Un compartimiento de segunda clase con elegantes sillones, que como el chat-bar, recrean la atmósfera de un lounge de una boutique de hotel.

Particolari di una vettura di seconda classe, con eleganti sedili e chat bars pensate per ricreare l'atmosfera intima del lounge di un hotel boutique.

The redesign of the original TGV was done by Christian Lacroix with an inspired bright purple and acid green scheme illustrated by the first-class cabin.

Christian Lacroix gestaltete den ursprünglichen TGV mit einer aufregend neuen Farbkombination aus leuchtendem Violett und grellem Grün neu, hier gezeigt in einem Erste-Klasse-Abteil.

Le nouveau design du TGV original a été dessiné par Christian Lacroix dans un accord de violet lumineux et de vert acide pour les cabines de première classe.

Christian Lacroix realizó el nuevo diseño de los TGV. Para los compartimentos de primera clase escogió los colores púrpura brillante y verde ácido.

Il restyling del TGV originale, opera di Christian Lacroix, è giocato su un accattivante accostamento cromatico tra viola e verde acido, come illustra la vettura di prima classe.

CHARACTERISTICS & AMENITIES	
Date built	2007
Compartments	—
Suites	—
Seats	360 (110 First class)
Restaurant capacity	bar on-board
Origin	Paris
Destination	Varied within East France, Luxembourg, and Germany, Switzerland
Itinerary	Varied within East France, Luxembourg, and Germany, Switzerland
Amenities (Services)	Power outlets, convertible game boards & floor space for children and office spaces

SHINKANSEN

The environmental superiority of the Shinkansen N700 is impressive due to its ability to simultaneously increase train output, improve performance, and enhance comfort and space. A significant reduction in CO_2 emissions and energy consumption makes the Shinkansen N700 one of the most environmentally-conscious trains in existence and its additional features, such as a quiet cabin and larger tables, make it one of the most business-friendly.

Die ökologische Überlegenheit des Shinkansen N700 ist besonders bemerkenswert, da er gleichzeitig Leistung, Komfort und den zur Verfügung stehenden Raum verbessert. Eine signifikante Verringerung des CO_2-Ausstoßes und des Energieverbrauchs lassen den Shinkansen N700 zu einem der umweltbewusstesten Züge der Welt werden. Seine ruhigen Abteile und größeren Tische machen ihn zudem besonders Business-freundlich.

Le Shinkansen N700 combine l'amélioration de la performance ainsi que celle du confort et de l'espace. Sa réduction significative des émissions de CO_2 et de sa consommation d'énergie fait du Shinkansen N700 un des trains les plus écologiques existants. D'autre part, il compte également parmi des ses caractéristiques supplémentaires, une cabine silencieuse et de plus grandes tables, en faisant un des train d'affaires les plus appréciés.

Una reducción de las emisiones de CO_2 y consumo de energía considerable hace del Shinkansen uno de los trenes más respetuosos del planeta con el medio ambiente. La superioridad medioambiental del Shinkansen N700 resulta impresionante, ya que ha sido capaz a su vez de aumentar la potencia, mejorar el rendimiento y el confort, y ampliar el espacio, a lo que se suman otros detalles como una cabina silenciosa o mesas más espaciosas, que le convierten en un tren ideal para los ejecutivos.

Lo Shinkansen N700 colpisce per la sua capacità di incrementare le prestazioni migliorando al contempo il comfort e lo spazio. La significativa riduzione delle emissioni di CO_2 e un risparmio energetico ne fanno inoltre uno dei treni più "ecologisti" sulla piazza. Caratteristiche accessorie come la silenziosità delle vetture e la disponibilità di piani d'appoggio più grandi lo rendono particolarmente adatto a chi viaggia per lavoro.

Businesspersons will greatly benefit from the Shinkansen's improved amenities such as larger tables to fit laptop computers and a significant increase in the number of power outlets on-board.

Geschäftsleute werden von den zahlreichen Verbesserungen des Shinkansen profitieren, wie z. B. von den größeren Tischen für Laptops und von deutlich mehr Steckdosen.

Les hommes d'affaires profitent de l'amélioration des aménagements du Shinkansen tels que de plus grandes tables correspondant aux ordinateurs portables et à une augmentation significative des prises électriques à bord.

Los ejecutivos se benefician ampliamente de las mejoras en los servicios que ofrece el Shinkansen, mesas más espaciosas que se adaptan al los ordenadores portátiles y un aumento significativo del número de tomas de corriente a bordo.

Gli uomini d'affari trarranno particolare beneficio dal miglioramento delle comodità a bordo dello Shinkansen, dai piani d'appoggio più grandi in grado di accogliere diversi computer portatili al notevole aumento delle prese di corrente.

Mount Fuji in the background

Im Hintergrund der Fuji

Le Mont Fuji à l'arrière plan

Al fondo el monte Fuji

Il Monte Fuji sullo sfondo

CHARACTERISTICS & AMENITIES	
Date built	2007
Compartments	Up to 16 cars
Suites	Only seating
Seats	200 first class (Green Car)
Restaurant capacity	No restaurant
Origin	Varied within Japan
Destination	Varied within Japan
Itinerary	Varied within Japan
Amenities (Services)	Non-smoking seats, power outlets, luggage rack, wireless Internet in 2009

ICE

The InterCityExpress has seen such success as a high-speed train in Germany that versions of the train have been bought by other countries as far away as China. The outstanding grey and red design of the exterior of the train is so popular that it has been registered as intellectual property. The interior too has been furbished to meet every need of the passengers, from electrical sockets to wireless internet and an on-board restaurant and bistro.

Der Hochgeschwindigkeitszug InterCityExpress war in Deutschland derart erfolgreich, dass selbst so ferne Länder wie China den Zug für sich bestellten. Sein auffallendes grau-rotes Äußeres ist so beliebt, dass es urheberrechtlich geschützt werden musste. Das Innere des Zuges befriedigt alle Bedürfnisse der Passagiere – von Steckdosen über WLAN bis zu Speisewagen und Bistro.

L'InterCityExpress a connu un tel succès comme train à grande vitesse en Allemagne que des versions du train ont été achetées par d'autres pays telle que la Chine. L'exceptionnel design gris et rouge de l'extérieur du train est si populaire qu'il a été breveté. L'intérieur a également été refait pour répondre à tous les besoins des passagers : des prises électriques à la connexion Internet sans fil au restaurant à bord et au bistrot.

El éxito del InterCityExpress como tren de alta velocidad en Alemania ha sido tan grande que países tan lejanos como China lo han adquirido. También su diseño exterior gris y rojo se ha hecho tan popular que ha sido registrado como propiedad intelectual. En el interior se han cuidado todos los detalles para satisfacer las necesidades de los pasajeros como enchufes eléctricos, Internet sin cable o restaurante y bar a bordo.

Tale è stato il successo riscosso in Germania dall'InterCityExpress che questo treno ad alta velocità è stato esportato in diversi paesi tra cui la Cina. La banda rossa e la scritta in grigio che lo contraddistinguono sono talmente entrate nell'immaginario da diventare un marchio registrato. Gli interni sono equipaggiati per soddisfare ogni esigenza dei passeggeri, dalle prese di corrente al collegamento Internet wireless, al ristorante e bar di bordo.

The ICE is the fastest train of the Deutsche Bahn AG traveling at up to 186 mph.

Der ICE ist mit seinen 300 km/h der schnellste Zug der Deutschen Bahn AG.

Le ICE est le train le plus rapide de la Deutsche Bahn AG, il roule à de 300 km/h.

El ICE es el tren más rápido de la Deutsche Bahn AG y puede alcanzar una velocidad de hasta 300 km/h.

Con la sua velocità massima di oltre 300 km/h, l'ICE è il treno più veloce della Deutsche Bahn AG.

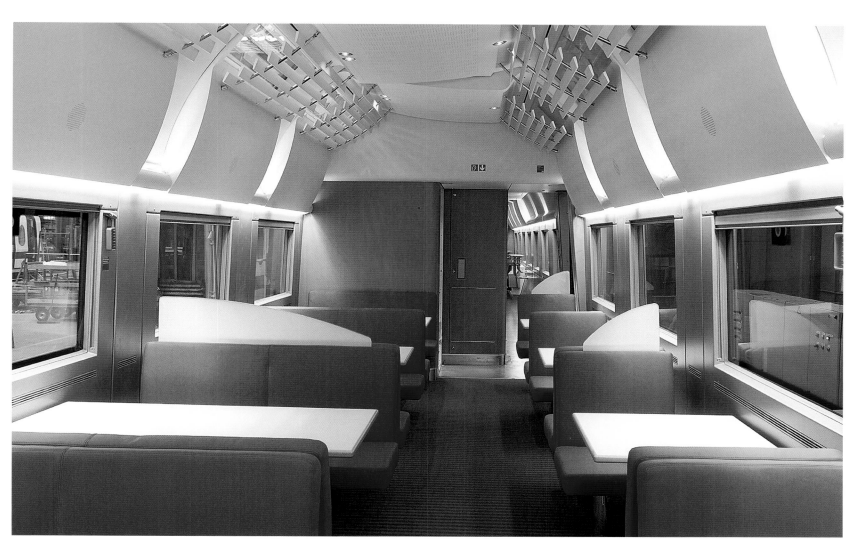

CHARACTERISTICS & AMENITIES

Date built	1991
Compartments	Between 4 and 12
Suites	Seating only
Seats	195 – 649
Restaurant capacity	—
Origin	Varied within Germany and neighboring countries
Destination	Varied within Germany, Austria, Switzerland, Belgium, Netherlands, and Denmark
Itinerary	Varied within Germany, Austria, Switzerland, Belgium, Netherlands, and Denmark
Amenities (Services)	Air-conditioning, on-board music, video displays, wireless Internet

X-2000

A first-class ticket on the Swedish X-2000 guarantees not only swift passage but a full meal on-board as well as wireless internet. Along with its more conventional carriages, the X-2000 carries a cinema carriage, playing some of the latest films. Selected classical music is piped in to first class via courtesy headphones as the train travels throughout the Swedish countryside radiating out from Stockholm.

Ein Ticket erster Klasse im schwedischen X-2000 bietet nicht nur eine schnelle Fahrt, sondern auch ein Menü und WLAN. Neben seinen konventionelleren Wagons führt der X-2000 auch einen Kinowagen mit sich, in dem die neuesten Filme gezeigt werden. In der Ersten Klasse kann man zudem klassischer Musik über die zur Verfügung gestellten Kopfhörer lauschen, während der Zug von Stockholm aus durch die schwedische Landschaft fährt.

Un billet de première classe pour le X-2000 suédois garantit non seulement un voyage rapide mais également un menu complet et une connexion Internet. En plus des conventionnels wagons, X-2000 comporte un wagon-cinéma, où sont projetés les dernières nouveautés. Une sélection de musique classique est diffusée en première classe à travers des casques audio alors que le train traverse la campagne suédoise en partance de Stockholm.

Un billete de primera clase en el Swedish X-2000 garantiza no solo rapidez sino también comida a bordo e Internet sin cable. Además de los vagones convencionales, el X-2000 dispone de un vagón cine que proyecta algunas de las películas más actuales. Gracias a auriculares sin cable el pasajero puede disfrutar de una selección de música clásica mientras el tren atraviesa los paisajes suecos dejando atrás la capital, Estocolmo.

Un biglietto di prima classe per lo svedese X-2000 non solo garantisce rapidità di spostamento ma dà diritto a un pasto completo a bordo e collegamento Internet wireless. Oltre ai vagoni più convenzionali, l'X-2000 propone una carrozza cinema dove vengono proiettati film in prima visione. La musica classica diffusa dalle cuffie in dotazione ai posti di prima classe accompagna i viaggiatori sulle varie tratte che, da Stoccolma, si diramano tra i paesaggi naturali scandinavi.

CHARACTERISTICS & AMENITIES	
Date built	1989 – 1998
Compartments	6 cars
Suites	—
Seats	261 – 309
Restaurant capacity	Bistro on-board
Origin	Varied within Sweden
Destination	Varied within Sweden and Denmark
Itinerary	Varied within Sweden and Copenhagen (Denmark)
Amenities (Services)	On-board bistro, cinema car, fax machine, wireless Internet, seat-to-seat trolley service, telephone-free compartment

AVE

AVE, Alta Velocidad Española, is the primary high-speed train within Spain and the only Spanish train to offer direct connections outside of the country. The train also offers music and video in all seats, traveling through Spain with the utmost comfort and quality service. The recent Series 103 is the fastest train in Europe and one of the fastest in the entire world.

AVE – Alta Velocidad Española – ist der erste Hochgeschwindigkeitszug innerhalb Spaniens und der einzige, der eine direkte Verbindung ins Ausland bietet. Auf allen Plätzen gibt es die Möglichkeit, Musik zu hören und Videos anzusehen, so dass man Spanien in höchster Annehmlichkeit und mit dem besten Service durchqueren kann. Die neueste Serie 103 ist der schnellste Zug Europas und einer der schnellsten der Welt.

L'AVE, Alta Velocidad Española, est le premier train espagnol à grande vitesse et le premier à proposer des connexions directes avec l'étranger. Le train offre musique et vidéos à chaque place. Il traverse l'Espagne dans le plus grand confort avec un service de qualité. La récente série 103 est le train le plus rapide d'Europe et un des plus rapides du monde.

AVE es el primer tren de alta velocidad español y el único en España que ofrece conexiones con el extranjero. El tren pone a disposición de los pasajeros música y proyecciones vídeo en todos los asientos y viaja por las latitudes españolas con el mayor confort y calidad de servicio. Los trenes de la reciente Serie 103 son los más rápidos en Europa y se encuentran entre los más rápidos del mundo.

AVE, Alta Velocidad Española, è il nome della principale rete spagnola di treni ad alta velocità, l'unica a offrire collegamenti diretti con destinazioni al di fuori del territorio nazionale. L'attraversamento delle alture iberiche si svolge nel massimo comfort e con elevata qualità di servizio, come dimostrato per esempio dai sedili equipaggiati con musica e video. I treni della recente serie 103 sono i più veloci d'Europa e tra i più veloci a livello mondiale.

First Class cabin

Kabine erster Klasse

Cabine de première classe

Cabina de primera clase

Cabina di prima classe

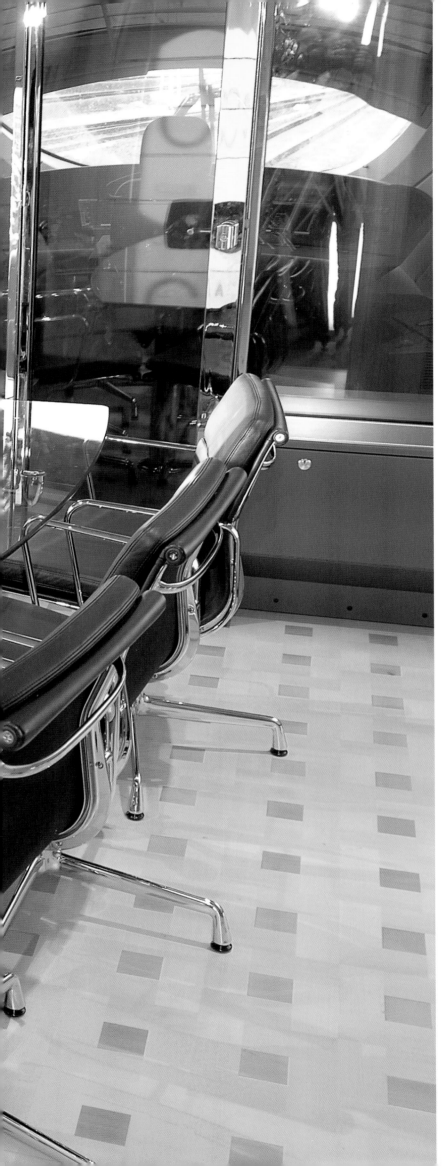

Club Class meeting room

Besprechungsraum der Club-Class

Salle de conférence Club Class

Sala de reuniones del Club Class

Sala riunioni della Club Class

CHARACTERISTICS & AMENITIES	
Date built	1992
Compartments	8 cars
Suites	Seating only
Seats	281 – 404
Restaurant capacity	On-board cafeteria
Origin	Varied within Spain
Destination	Varied within Spain
Itinerary	Varied within Spain
Amenities (Services)	business room, air conditioning, heating

GLACIER EXPRESS

The Glacier Express prides itself on being the world's slowest fast train in its journey through the glacier landscapes and unspoilt natural beauty of the Swiss Alps. The panoramic windows of the carriages were specially designed for the train to ensure that its slow speed is every bit worth the view. To cope with the steep slopes of the mountains, the Glacier Express has even released its own special tilted wine glass, now a popular collector's item. The Glacier Express is also equipped to handle the extreme weathers traveling with a plow able to move 19 tons of snow per minute.

Der Glacier Express ist stolz darauf, der langsamste Schnellzug der Welt zu sein. Er fährt durch die Gletscherlandschaften und die unberührte Natur der Schweizer Alpen. Die Panoramafenster der Wagen wurden extra für den Zug entworfen, damit man die Ausblicke während der langsamen Fahrt auch tatsächlich zu würdigen weiß. Um auch auf steilen Abhängen in Ruhe genießen zu können, wurden spezielle verkantete Weingläser entwickelt, die inzwischen ein beliebtes Sammelobjekt darstellen. Der Glacier Express hält auch extremem Wetter stand und kann mit seinem Pflug pro Minute 19 Tonnen Schnee beiseite räumen.

L'Express de Glaciar qui traverse les grands glaciers et toute la beauté des Alpes suisses peut s'enorgueillir d'être le train rapide le plus lent du monde. Les fenêtres panoramiques des voitures ont été spécialement conçues en fonction de la vitesse du train pour que chaque vue puissent être profitée au maximum. Pour contrer les pentes raides des montagnes, l'Express de Glacier a même imaginé un verre de vin penché, aujourd'hui objet de collection populaire. Le Glacier Express est aussi équipé, pour les temps extrêmes, d'une charrue capable de déplacer 19 tonnes de neige par minute.

El Glacier Express se enorgullece de ser el más lento de los trenes rápidos que viaja a través de los paisajes glaciales y la belleza natural y virgen de los Alpes suizos. Aunque las ventanas panorámicas de los vagones han sido diseñadas especialmente para asegurar que las vistas compensen con creces la baja velocidad del tren. Para salvar las consecuencias derivadas de las pendientes abruptas de las montañas, el Glacier Express también ha diseñado su propia copa de vino, que ya se ha convertido en un objeto popular para coleccionistas. El Glacier Express está equipado para poder soportar condiciones climáticas extremas con unas palas que pueden mover hasta 19 toneladas de nieve por minuto.

Il Glacier Express, che accompagna i passeggeri tra i paesaggi innevati e le bellezze della natura incontaminata delle Alpi svizzere, si vanta di essere il treno rapido più lento del mondo. I finestrini panoramici delle carrozze sono stati appositamente progettati in modo che alla bassa velocità del convoglio corrispondano le visuali più suggestive. Per gustare al meglio un sorso di buon vino durante le ripide risalite del percorso, il Glacier Express dispone di speciale bicchieri inclinati, divenuti ormai popolari oggetti da collezione. Il Glacier Express è inoltre pronto a fronteggiare anche le condizioni atmosferiche più estreme, essendo equipaggiato di sgombraneve centrifughi in grado di soffiare via 19 tonnellate di neve al minuto.

Bizarre rock formations seams the way of the Glacier Express in the Ruinaulta, the Rhine ravine, known as the "Swiss Grand Canyon."

Bizarre Felsformationen säumen den Weg des Glacier Express durch die Rheinschlucht Ruinaulta, auch bekannt als der „Schweizer Grand Canyon".

Des formations de roches étranges trace la voie du Glacier Express à travers le Ruinaulta, les gorges du Rhin, plus connu sous le nom de « Grand Canyon suisse ».

Peculiares formaciones rocosas dan paso al camino del Glacier Express en el Ruinaulta, el barranco del Rin, también conocido como el "Gran Cañón Suizo."

Bizzarre formazioni rocciose accompagnano il cammino del Glacier Express attraverso la Ruinaulta, la gola del Reno, detta anche il "Grand Canyon svizzero".

CHARACTERISTICS & AMENITIES	
Date built	1930
Compartments	5 – 6
Suites	–
Seats	36 – 54 seats per car
Restaurant capacity	34 – 60 passengers
Origin	Zermatt
Destination	St. Moritz
Itinerary	Zermatt – Brig – Andermatt – Disentis – St. Moritz
Amenities (Services)	Air-conditioning, catering services, railbar, service at your seat

TANGULA

From April 2009, the Tangula Luxury Train will speed along an unprecedented journey through remote landscapes of China. A sense of exclusivity is preserved throughout the passage with only 96 guests on board and only four suites to a car, leaving spacious carriages for all to enjoy. Passengers traverse the Silk Road and pass by Tibetan plateaus as they dine on exquisite meals prepared exclusively by Tangula's Executive Chef.

Ab April 2009 wird der Tangula Luxuszug eine bisher beispiellose Route durch ferne chinesische Landschaften nehmen. Ein Gefühl von Exklusivität wird allein durch die Tatsache entstehen, dass nur 96 Gäste an Bord sind und es bloß vier Suiten pro Wagen und somit genügend Platz gibt. Die Passagiere überqueren die Seidenstraße und passieren tibetische Hochebenen, während sie exquisite Speisen zu sich nehmen, die vom Chefkoch des Tangula zubereitet werden.

À partir d'avril 2009, le Tangula Luxury Train parcourera à travers les lointains paysages de la Chine dans un voyage sans précédent. L'exclusivité du séjour est préservée grâce à un nombre d'invités limité à 96 et à quatre uniques suites d'une voiture, laissant ainsi les spacieux wagons à l'usage de tous. Les passagers empruntent la route de la Soie et passent par les hauts plateaux tibétains où ils pourront goûter des plats exquis préparés en exclusivité par le chef cuisinier du Tangula.

A partir de abril 2009, el Tangula Luxury Train inaugurará un trayecto sin precedentes a través de paisajes remotos de China. Sus promotores han querido dotar al tren de una sensación de exclusividad, ya que tiene capacidad para acoger a tan solo 96 pasajeros a bordo, y solamente hay cuatro suites por vagón, para que los viajeros disfruten de coches espaciosos. El tren atraviesa la ruta de la seda y las mesetas tibetanas mientras los invitados degustan exquisitos platos preparados exclusivamente por el Chef a bordo.

Il Tangula Luxury Train ha aperto percorsi senza precedenti nelle più remote regioni della Cina. La sensazione di esclusività è ribadita dal numero limitato di viaggiatori (96) e di suite per carrozza (4), con spaziosi vagoni completamente dedicati all'intrattenimento degli ospiti. I passeggeri del Tangula hanno l'occasione di percorrere la Via della Seta o attraversare l'altopiano del Tibet gustando i prelibati piatti appositamente preparati dallo chef di bordo.

To ensure maximum comfort, the trains have an on-board oxygen enrichment system allowing guests to travel at ease at altitudes about three miles.

Um maximalen Komfort zu bieten, haben die Züge eine Sauerstoffanreicherungsanlage, die es den Gästen ermöglicht, auch auf Höhen von bis zu 5.000 Metern bequem zu reisen.

Pour garantir un confort maximal, les trains possèdent un système denrichissement en oxygène intégré permettant aux invités de voyager en toutes commodités à environ 5000 m d'altitude.

Para asegurar un máximo confort el tren tiene un sistema de oxígeno a bordo que permite a los pasajeros viajar cómodamente a una altitud de 5000 m aproximadamente.

Il Tangula è fornito di un impianto di ossigenazione che permette ai passeggeri di superare nel massimo comfort e relax gli oltre 5000 m di altitudine toccati dal treno.

CHARACTERISTICS & AMENITIES	
Date built	2009
Compartments	12 suite cars, 2 dining cars, 1 lounge car
Suites	4 suites per car, 2 passengers per suite
Seats	96
Restaurant capacity	96
Origin	Beijing
Destination	Lhasa or Lijiang
Itinerary	Northern Route: Beijing – Lhasa Southern Route: Beijing – Lijiang
Amenities (Services)	Private bathroom, room service, mini bar, television, wireless Internet, wardrobe, writing desk, hairdryer, personal safe

THE ROYAL SCOTSMAN

BREAKFAST

Squeezed Orange Juice
it Compôte
pefruit
Yoghurt

EXCELLENCE
ON BOARD

EXCELLENCE ON BOARD

The allure of rail travel does not stop at the lavish décor or optimal comfort. The delectable meals prepared by world-renowned chefs and stewards dressed in immaculate uniforms enhance the experience and prestige aboard a luxury train. Each train provides constant steward service for all their guests catering to all their needs. Passengers can also enjoy the gastronomic splendor while trying different cuisines prepared with the freshest vegetables, meats, and fishes.

Zur Faszination des Bahnfahrens gehören nicht nur üppige Ausstattung und optimaler Komfort. Auch die köstlichen Speisen, die von weltbekannten Köchen zubereitet und von Stewards in makellosen Uniformen serviert werden, steigern das Erlebnis einer Reise im Luxuszug. Jeder Zug bietet einen ständigen Stewardservice für die Gäste und ihre Bedürfnisse an. Man kann die verschiedensten Gaumenfreuden genießen, stets aus frischstem Gemüse, Fleisch und Fisch.

L'attrait du voyage sur rail ne s'arrête pas au décor ou au confort. Les repas raffinés préparés par les grands chefs de renommée internationale et les stewards habillés en uniformes immaculés améliorent l'expérience et le prestige à bord d'un train de luxe. Chaque train fournit un service constant de steward à tous leurs invités répondant à chacun de leurs besoins. Les passagers peuvent aussi profiter de la gastronomique et essayer différentes cuisines préparées à base de légumes frais et des meilleurs viandes et poisson.

El encanto de viajar en tren no se limita solo a una decoración refinada y un confort óptimo. Platos deliciosos preparados por chefs de gran renombre y el personal ataviado con uniformes inmaculados realzan la experiencia y el prestigio de viajar en un tren de lujo. Todos los trenes disponen de un servicio permanente para los pasajeros que cuida todas sus necesidades. Los viajeros también pueden disfrutar de una magnífica variedad gastronómica probando diferentes tipos de cocina preparados a base de las verduras, las hortalizas, las carnes y los pescados más frescos.

Il fascino di un viaggio in treno non si limita alla preziosità degli arredi e agli elevati standard di comfort. Il prestigio di un treno di lusso è tipicamente associato anche alla presenza di steward in livrea e ai piatti appositamente preparati da chef di fama mondiale: ogni treno fornisce infatti un servizio di assistenza continuata volto a soddisfare qualsiasi esigenza del passeggero e mette a disposizione dei propri ospiti squisite pietanze provenienti da tradizioni gastronomiche diverse e preparate con le verdure, la carne e il pesce più freschi.

Venice Simplon

The Majestic Imperators' fourgon features a large, modern kitchen with large walk-in refrigerator for full catering services.

Zum Fourgon des Majestic Imperator gehört eine große, moderne Küche mit begehbarem Kühlschrank, um beste Bewirtung zu garantieren.

Le fourgon Majestic Imperator comporte une grande et moderne cuisine avec grand réfrigérateur plain-pied pour services intégraux de restauration.

El furgón del Majestic Imperator dispone de una amplia y moderna cocina con una cámara de refrigeración para servicios de catering completos.

In questa carrozza del Majestic Imperator vi è posto per un'ampia e moderna cucina con un capiente frigorifero accessibile per garantire un servizio ottimale.

Meals prepared by top chefs are served in the vintage Craigellachie dining car aboard the Royal Canadian Pacific.

Im klassischen Craigellachie-Speisewagen an Bord des Royal Canadian Pacific werden Gerichte von Spitzenköchen serviert.

Les repas préparés par des chefs de cuisine renommés sont servis dans la voiture-restaurant d'époque Craigellachie à bord du Royal Canadian Pacific.

Los platos preparados por los chefs más sobresalientes son servidos en el vagón comedor Craigellachie de estilo vintage a bordo del Royal Canadian Pacific.

Nella classica carrozza ristorante Craigellachie a bordo del Royal Canadian Pacific si servono piatti preparati dai migliori chef.

left: Light lunch served at the Rovos Rail

Leichtes Mittagessen an Bord der Rovos Rail

Déjeuner léger servi au Rovos Rail

Almuerzo ligero servido en el Rovos Rail

Un pranzo leggero viene servito a bordo del Rovos Rail

All Royal Canadian Pacific dishes are made with fresh Canadian ingredients.

Alle Speisen an Bord des Royal Canadian Pacific werden aus frischen kanadischen Zutaten zubereitet.

Tous les plats du Royal Canadian Pacific sont cuisinés avec des ingrédients canadiens frais.

Los platos del Royal Canadian Pacific se elaboran con ingredientes frescos canadienses.

Tutte le pietanze a bordo del Royal Canadian Pacific sono preparate con ingredienti freschi di origine canadese.

A steward prepares to disembark the Venice Simplon-Orient-Express.

Ein Steward beim Aussteigen aus dem Venice Simplon-Orient-Express.

Un steward prépare le débarquement du Venice Simplon-Orient-Express.

Un azafato se dispone para el desembarque del Venice Simplon-Orient-Express.

Uno steward si prepara a scendere dal Venice Simplon-Orient-Express.

The Royal Canadian Pacific hospitality staff greet guests as they board the train.

Die Service-Mitarbeiter des Royal Canadian Pacific begrüßen die Gäste beim Einsteigen.

Le personnel d'accueil du Royal Canadian Pacific salue les invités pendant qu'ils montent à bord du train.

El hospitalario personal del Royal Canadian Pacific da la bienvenida a los pasajeros que suben a bordo del tren.

Il personale del Royal Canadian Pacific accoglie gli ospiti mentre salgono sul treno.

top and page 150: British Pullman

opposite page: An Orient Express steward delivers afternoon tea to a compartment. Each compartment has a steward who is always available to tend to its needs. The steward will take care of passengers' passports, perform a turndown service to prepare cabins for day and night, and serve breakfast and afternoon tea.

Ein Steward des Orient Express serviert den Nachmittagstee in einem Abteil. Jedes Abteil verfügt über einen Steward, der stets erreichbar ist. Der Steward kümmert sich um die Reisepässe der Gäste, baut die Kabinen jeweils für die Nacht und den Tag um und serviert Frühstück sowie Nachmittagstee.

Un serveur livre chaque cabine le thé de l'après-midi. Chaque compartiment a son propre personnel à son entière disposition. Le serveur se charge des passeports des passagers, gère la préparation des cabines de jour et de nuit, et sert le petit déjeuner et le goûter.

Un azafato del Orient Express sirve el té de la tarde en un compartimiento. Cada compartimiento tiene un miembro del personal asignado, que está siempre disponible para atender a sus necesidades, como encargarse de los pasaportes, preparar el compartimiento para la noche o el día o servir el desayuno y el té de la tarde.

Un inserviente serve il tè in uno scompartimento. Ogni scompartimento ha un inserviente a completa disposizione degli ospiti. L'inserviente si occupa dei passaporti dei passeggeri, prepara le cabine per il giorno e per la notte e serve la colazione e il tè pomeridiano.

Venice Simplon

SPLENDID STATIONS

SPLENDID STATIONS

The luxury of the journey begins before the passengers even set foot on the train, from the moment they enter the station. Each of these elaborate and ornate buildings was designed to ensure a smooth start to a one-of-a-kind trip. Many are not only hubs of travel, they also include exquisite restaurants and shops and have been constructed by world-renowned architects. These stations begin and end the journey right—with the kind of service and splendour provided by the trains.

Der Luxus der Reise beginnt, noch ehe die Passagiere einen Fuß in den Zug gesetzt haben. Er beginnt mit dem Eintreffen im Bahnhof. Jedes dieser kunstvollen Gebäude wurde als reibungsloser Ausgangspunkt einer einzigartigen Reise entworfen. Viele stellen nicht nur Verkehrsknoten dar, sondern bieten auch exklusive Restaurants und Geschäfte und wurden von weltbekannten Architekten entwickelt. In diesen Bahnhöfen beginnt und endet eine Reise genau richtig – mit einem ähnlichen Service und Luxus wie in den Zügen selbst.

À peine le pied posé dans le train, le luxe du voyage commence lorsque le voyageur entre dans la gare. Chaque édifice de part son élaboration et sa décoration est conçu pour faire du voyage dès ses débuts une expérience unique. Nombreuses sont donc celles étant bien plus qu'un simple moyen de transport. Elles incluent des restaurants raffinés, des boutiques et ont été conçus par des architectes de renommée internationale. Ces gares marquent le début et la fin des voyages – avec un service et une élégance fournis par les trains.

El lujo de un viaje empieza antes de que los pasajeros embarquen en el tren, en el momentos mismo en que franquean la puerta de la estación. Estos edificios ricamente ornamentados han sido diseñados para asegurar una tranquila partida para cualquier tipo de viaje. Algunos no son tan solo áreas de tránsito sino que también disponen de restaurantes exquisitos y establecimientos comerciales, y han sido construidos por arquitectos de renombre mundial. Estas estaciones brindan el mismo servicio y esplendor al comienzo y final del viaje que los que el viajero en-cuentra en los trenes.

Prima ancora che il passeggero abbia messo piede sul treno, il tono e la preziosità di un viaggio sono dettati nel momento stesso in cui si arriva in stazione. Ciascuno degli elaborati ed eleganti edifici qui presentati è stato progettato per far sì che un viaggio unico e irripetibile abbia l'inizio più consono. Molte di queste stazioni non sono soltanto nodi di traffico, ma ospitano negozi e ristoranti esclusivi e sono opera di celeberrimi architetti. Qui il viaggio inizia e termina nel migliore dei modi, con lo stesso standard di servizio e livello di lusso garantito a bordo del treno.

Berlin Hauptbahnhof

BERLIN HAUPTBAHNHOF
BERLIN

As the largest two-level railway station in Europe, the modern design of Berlin's main station, Berlin Hauptbahnhof, covers over 750,000 square feet of floor space, about 160,000 square feet of which is dedicated to shops and restaurants. The initial design of the building aimed to make travel as smooth as possible for visitors and to fill the entire structure with natural light by constructing the halls from sheets of glass.

Berlins Hauptbahnhof ist der größte zweistöckige Bahnhof Europas. Das moderne Gebäude umfasst eine Fläche von 70.000 m^2, wovon etwa 15.000 m^2 für Geschäfte und Restaurants reserviert sind. Der Bahnhof wurde so geplant, dass die Abläufe für die Reisenden so angenehm wie möglich verlaufen, während das ganze Gebäude von Tageslicht erfüllt wird, das durch die Glashallen hereinfällt.

En tant que plus grande gare de chemin de fer de deux niveaux en Europe, la gare principale de Berlin, Berlin Hauptbahnhof, couvre 70 000 m^2 au sol, dont 15 000 m^2 dévoué aux magasins et aux restaurants. Le design initial du bâtiment a été conçu dans le but de rendre le voyage aussi tranquille que possible pour les passagers et de remplir au maximum la structure entière de lumière naturelle, en construisant les halls à partir de draps de verre.

El moderno diseño de la estación central de Berlín, Berlin Hauptbahnhof, la más grande de las de dos plantas de Europa, tiene una superficie de 70.000 m^2, de los cuales 15.000 m^2 están dedicados a restaurantes y establecimientos comerciales. El diseño inicial del edificio tenía como objetivo hacer que el viaje fuera lo más tranquilo posible para los visitantes y llenar la estructura entera del edificio de luz natural, construyendo las salas con láminas de vidrio.

Oltre che stazione centrale di Berlino, la Berlin Hauptbahnhof è la più grande stazione ferroviaria a due livelli d'Europa. Essa copre infatti una superficie di 70.000 m^2, circa 15.000 m^2 dei quali occupati da negozi e ristoranti, grazie a un moderno progetto che fin dall'inizio si è posto l'obiettivo di rendere il viaggio il più piacevole possibile per i passeggeri. L'impiego del vetro permette di inondare l'intero volume di luce naturale.

GARE DE LYON
PARIS

Originally built for the World Exposition of 1900, the architecture of the Gare De Lyon station in Paris is representative of the style of its time. The main clock tower above the corner of the station echos Big Ben of the United Kingdom's Houses of Parliament. The station is home to world-renowned restaurant, Le Train Bleu, a restaurant which has been serving travelers since 1901 in its ornate halls. The beauty of the station and its amenities offers visitors a sense of luxury and style along their journeys.

Ursprünglich für die Weltausstellung von 1900 erbaut, ist die Architektur des Gare de Lyon in Paris typisch für den Stil der Zeit. Der Uhrenturm über der Bahnhofsecke erinnert an den Londoner Big Ben. Im Bahnhof befindet sich das weltberühmte Restaurant Le Train Bleu, das seit 1901 Reisende in seinen üppigen Räumen bedient. Die Schönheit des Bahnhofs und seine Annehmlichkeiten vermitteln dem Besucher auf seiner Reise ein Gefühl von Luxus und Stil.

Construit à l'origine pour l'Exposition Universelle de 1900, la Gare de Lyon est tout à fait représentative du style de l'époque. La tour de l'horloge principale ornant la gare rappelle le Big Ben du siège du Parlement britannique. La gare a également une renommée internationale grâce à l'ornementation fastueuse du restaurant Le Train Bleu en fonction depuis 1901. La beauté de la gare et de ses équipements offrent aux visiteurs luxe et élégance au cours de leurs voyages.

Originalmente construido para la Exposición Universal de 1900, la arquitectura de la Gare de Lyon en París es representativa del estilo de esa época. La torre del reloj principal, que se eleva sobre una de las esquinas de la estación, está inspirada en la del Big Ben del Parlamento Británico en Reino Unido. La estación hospeda un restaurante de renombre mundial, Le Train Bleu. Desde 1901 este restaurante ha servido a los viajeros en sus salones ornamentados. La belleza de la estación y sus servicios ofrecen a los visitantes un ambiente de lujo y estilo en sus desplazamientos.

Costruita in occasione dell'Esposizione Universale del 1900, la Gare de Lyon a Parigi riflette nella sua architettura lo stile dell'epoca. Un'estremità della facciata principale è dominata dalla torre dell'orologio, che ricorda il Big Ben del Palazzo del Parlamento di Londra. La stazione ospita il rinomato Le Train Bleu, un ristorante dagli interni riccamente decorati attivo fin dal 1901. La bellezza della stazione e delle sue strutture accessorie trasmette ai passeggeri una sensazione di lusso che li accompagnerà per tutto il viaggio.

The station hosts trains from various transit systems that generally run to the south and east of France, but due to modernized engineering the station also provides transportation through TGV Trains to the Alps, Basel/Switzerland, and Rome/Italy.

Auf dem Bahnhof finden sich Züge aus vielen Schienenverkehrsnetzen ein, die meist in den Süden und Osten Frankreichs weiterfahren. Doch seit der Modernisierung bietet der Bahnhof auch die Möglichkeit, mit TGV-Zügen in die Alpen, nach Basel und nach Rom zu reisen.

La gare accueille des trains de différentes provenances traversant généralement le sud et l'est de la France. En raison de sa modernisation, elle dessert également les TGV allant vers les Alpes, Bâle en Suisse ainsi que Rome en Italie.

La estación alberga trenes de diversos tipos que por lo general se dirigen al Este y Sur de Francia. Pero gracias a la ingeniería modernizada de la estación, también forma parte de los trayectos de los trenes TGV con destino a los Alpes y Basilea en Suiza, y a Roma, en Italia.

La stazione accoglie treni in servizio su reti ferroviarie diverse e che in genere percorrono le tratte verso il sud e l'est della Francia. L'ammodernamento degli impianti ha consentito tuttavia di offrire anche il trasporto ad alta velocità, TGV, con destinazione Roma, Basilea e le Alpi.

pages 166 – 169: Le Train Bleu Restaurant

AVIGNON GARE TGV
AVIGNON

Built on the line of the TGV Mediterranean, the Avignon TGV train station was completed in 2001 under the architectural planning and guidance of Jean Marie Duthilleul and Jean François Blassel. The contemporary design of the station contradicts the majority of the architecture of Vaucluse. The layout of the station instead parallels the landscape of the region's countryside. Housed in glass and steel, the construction of the station protects traveler's from seasonal winds while maintaining an aesthetic appeal.

Der TGV-Bahnhof Avignon, der sich auf der Strecke des TGV Méditerranée befindet, wurde 2001 unter der architektonischen Leitung von Jean Marie Duthilleul und Jean François Blassel fertiggestellt. Das zeitgemäße Design steht im Gegensatz zur Architektur des Vaucluse. Der Bahnhof richtet sich stattdessen an der Landschaft der Region aus. Aus Glas und Stahl bestehend, schützt das Gebäude den Reisenden vor Wind und strahlt gleichzeitig eine große Ästhetik aus.

Construit sur la ligne du TGV Méditerranée, la gare TGV d'Avignon a été achevée en 2001 sur les plans de Jean Marie Duthilleul et de Jean François Blassel. Le design de la gare contraste avec l'architecture habituelle du Vaucluse, mais la disposition de la gare ressemble au paysage de la campagne de la région. Le choix esthétique des matériaux de construction le verre et l'acier protège de plus le voyageur des vents saisonniers.

La estación de TGV de Avignon fue construida en 2001, en la ruta del TGV del Mediterráneo, bajo la dirección de los arquitectos Jean Marie Duthilleul y Jean François Blassel. El diseño contemporáneo de la estación contrasta con la arquitectura dominante del departamento de Vaucluse, en cambio se asimila a los paisajes de la región. Realizada en acero y vidrio, la construcción de la estación cumple una doble función, por un lado protege al viajero de los vientos estacionales, y por otra, actúa como reclamo estético.

Costruita sulla linea LGV Méditerranée, la stazione di Avignone è stata completata nel 2001 con la supervisione dei progettisti Jean Marie Duthilleul e Jean François Blassel. Il disegno contemporaneo della stazione si pone in contrasto con la maggior parte dell'architettura della Vaucluse, richiamando piuttosto il paesaggio della regione. Con il suo involucro di vetro e acciaio, l'edificio protegge i viaggiatori dai venti stagionali conservando al tempo stesso un significativo valore estetico.

Wood, glass, concrete and steel have been used for the decoration.

Für die Innenausstattung wurden Holz, Glas, Beton und Stahl verwendet.

Bois, verre, béton et acier ont été employés pour la décoration.

Madera, vidrio, hormigón y acero son los materiales empleados en la decoración.

Per gli interni sono stati impiegati legno, vetro, cemento e acciaio.

SOUTHERN CROSS STATION
MELBOURNE

Southern Cross Station, formerly Spencer Street Station, is the hub of all V/Line Trains in the whole of Australia—all the trains and most of the coaches depart from here. Recently renovated by famed architect Sir Nicholas Grimshaw, the station now bears a distinctive, wave-shaped roof and several new modern terminals, platforms, and a shopping complex. The station has since been awarded the Lubetkin Prize from the Royal Institute of British Architects for the most outstanding building outside the European Union.

Der Bahnhof Southern Cross – ursprünglich Spencer Street Station – ist der Verkehrsknotenpunkt der V/Line-Züge aus ganz Australien. Alle Züge und fast alle Busse starten von hier. Vor kurzem von dem berühmten Architekten Sir Nicholas Grimshaw umgebaut, weist der Bahnhof nun ein auffallendes, wellenförmiges Dach und mehrere moderne Terminals, Bahnsteige und einen Geschäftskomplex auf. Er wurde mit dem Lubetkin-Preis des Royal Institute of British Architects für das außergewöhnlichste Gebäude außerhalb Europas ausgezeichnet.

La Southern Cross Station, autrefois Spencer Street Station, est le point de départ de toutes les V/Line en Australie – tous les trains et la plupart des bus partent d'ici. Récemment rénovée par le célèbre architecte Nicholas Grimshaw, la gare porte maintenant un nouveau toit distinctif , plusieurs nouveaux terminaux, des quais et un centre commercial. La gare a reçu le prix Lubetkin du Royal Institute of British Architects pour le bâtiment le plus exceptionnel à l'extérieur de l'Union Européenne.

La Southern Cross Station, antiguamente llamada Spencer Street Station, es el punto de partida de todos los trenes y la mayoría de autocares de Australia. Renovada recientemente por el famoso arquitecto Sir Nicholas Grimshaw, la estación ahora se distingue por un peculiar tejado ondulado, varias terminales nuevas, andenes y un complejo comercial. Southern Cross Station ha sido galardonada con el Lubetkin Prize por el Royal Institute of British Architects como edificio más destacado fuera de la Unión Europea.

La Southern Cross Station di Melbourne, un tempo Spencer Street Station, è il nodo in cui confluiscono tutti i treni della compagnia australiana V/Line. Tutti i treni e la maggior parte delle corriere parte da qui. Ristrutturata di recente dal celebre architetto Nicholas Grimshaw, la stazione ora sfoggia un caratteristico tetto ondulato, un complesso commerciale, diversi nuovi e più moderni binari e terminali. Il progetto ha vinto il Lubetkin Prize del Royal Institute of British Architects come edificio più interessante fuori dai confini dell'Unione Europea.

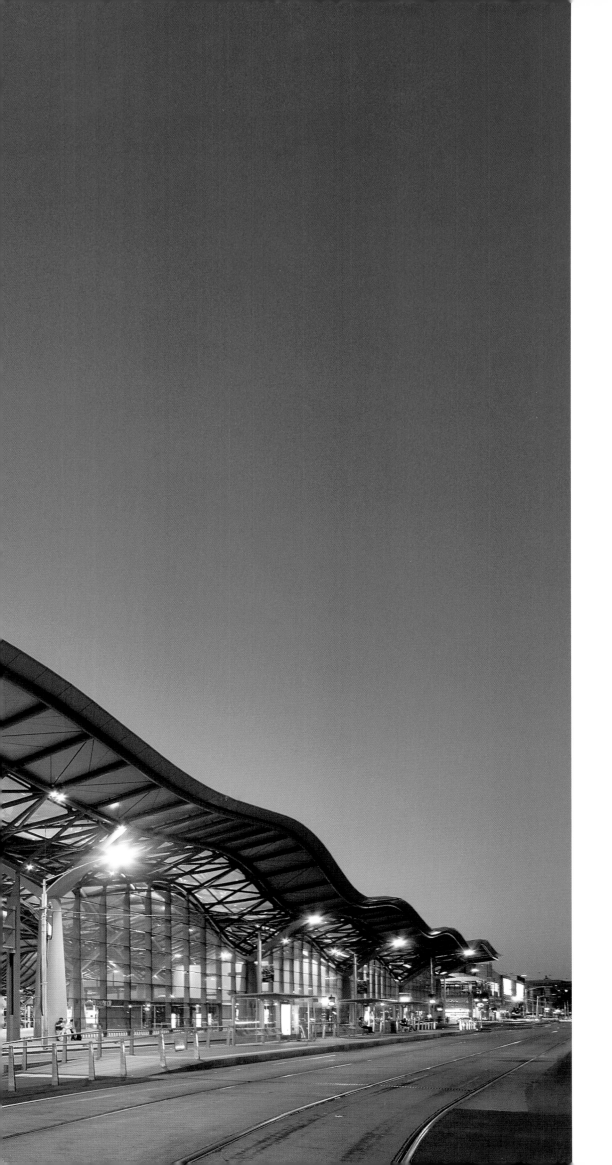

The newly refurnished Southern Cross Station provides the 15 million users per annum.

Im neu gestalteten Bahnhof Southern Cross werden jährlich 15 Millionen Reisende abgefertigt.

La gare nouvellement modernisée de Southern Cross Station traite 15 millions de passagers par an.

La estación renovada de Southern Cross acoge cada año 15 millones de pasajeros.

La rinnovata Southern Cross Station accoglie ogni anno 15 milioni di passeggeri.

The roof system is devised from complex geometry, with no repetition or symmetry.

Der Dachkonstruktion liegt eine komplexe Geometrie zugrunde, die weder Wiederholungen noch Symmetrie zulässt.

Le système de la toiture est conçu avec une géométrie complexe, sans aucune répétition ni symétrie.

El sistema del tejado se compone de una compleja geometría, sin repeticiones ni simetrias.

La copertura è contraddistinta da una complessa geometria, priva di simmetrie e ripetizioni.

BIJLMER ARENA STATION
AMSTERDAM

After renovations by architect Sir Nicholas Grimshaw, the Amsterdam Bijlmer ArenA Station is one of the five largest stations in the Netherlands. With the renovations, the station has doubled its tracks. The roof, the most striking feature of the new station, emphasizes the flow of traffic within and allows for daylight to stream inside.

Nach den Umbauten durch den Architekten Sir Nicholas Grimshaw gehört der Amsterdamer Bijlmer ArenA Bahnhof zu den fünf größten der Niederlande. Seitdem gibt es doppelt so viele Gleise wie früher. Das Dach, das beim neuen Bahnhof am meisten ins Auge sticht, betont den Verkehrsfluss im Inneren und lässt Tageslicht von außen hineinströmen.

Après les rénovations de l'architecte Nicholas Grimshaw, l'Amsterdam Bijlmer ArenA Station est une des cinq plus grandes gares aux Pays-Bas. Depuis, la gare a doublé son nombre de quais. Le toit, la caractéristique la plus frappante de la nouvelle gare, accentue le flux de circulation à l'intérieur et laissant entrer la lumière du jour sous forme de ruisseau à l'intérieur.

Después de las renovaciones llevadas a cabo por el arquitecto Sir Nicholas Grimshaw, la estación Amsterdam Bijlmer ArenA se ha convertido en una de las cinco más grandes de Holanda. Con estas reformas, la estación ha doblado su número de vías. El techo, el elemento más sobresaliente de la estación, enfatiza la corriente de tráfico y permite la entrada de la luz solar.

Dopo i lavori di ristrutturazione diretti dall'architetto Nicholas Grimshaw, la Bijlmer ArenA Station di Amsterdam è oggi una delle cinque maggiori stazioni olandesi, avendo raddoppiato il numero di binari. La copertura, elemento di maggiore attrattiva della nuova stazione, pone l'accento sui flussi di traffico sottostanti, lasciando filtrare la luce naturale all'interno della struttura.

The Bijlmer station required a substantial expansion and renovation, including the addition of four railtracks and a metro stop.

Beim Bijlmer Bahnhof waren Renovierungsarbeiten und eine deutliche Erweiterung nötig, u. a. die vier zusätzlichen Gleise und eine Metrostation.

La gare de Bijlmer a subi une expansion et une rénovation substantielles, y compris l'addition de quatre voies ferroviaires et un arrêt du métro.

La estación Bijlmer requería una extensión y una renovación substanciales, que incluían cuatro nuevas vías y una parada de metro.

La Bijlmer ha richiesto notevoli interventi di ampliamento e ristrutturazione, tra cui l'aggiunta di quattro binari e di una stazione della metropolitana.

Combining aesthetics with functionality, the Bijlmer station provides a feeling of transparency and lightness, and also comfort and safety.

Der Bijlmer Bahnhof verbindet Ästhetik mit Funktionalität und vermittelt das Gefühl von Transparenz, Leichtigkeit, Komfort und Sicherheit.

Combinant l'esthétique avec la fonctionnalité, la gare de Bijlmer fournit un sentiment de transparence et de légèreté, et également confort et sécurité.

Conjugando estética y funcionalidad, la estación Bijlmer transmite una sensación de transparencia y ligereza al mismo tiempo que confort y seguridad.

Coniugando estetica e funzionalità, la Bijlmer trasmette una sensazione di leggerezza e trasparenza, ma anche di comfort e sicurezza.

An impressive steel, glass and wood roof lets daylight into the station, creating an inviting experience for travelers. The base-element of the roof structure is a "V" shaped continuous hollow steel boom with steel arms cantilevered on either side to support all the roof glazing.

Durch ein beeindruckendes Dach aus Stahl, Glas und Holz fällt Tageslicht in den Bahnhof, so dass dieser besonders einladend wirkt. Das Grundelement des Daches ist ein hohler Stahlträger in Form eines V, von dem aus freitragende Stahlarme in beide Richtungen ausgreifen, um das Glasdach zu tragen.

Le toit de verre et de bois et l'impressionnante structure en acier laisse passer la lumière du jour dans la gare créant une atmosphère acceuillante. L'élément de base en forme de V est une estacade en acier creux de laquelle partent des poutres également en acier supportant l'ensemble du toit de verre.

Un techo impresionante de acero, madera y vidrio deja que la luz natural se filtre en la estación, propi ciando una agradable sensación a los viajeros. El elemento base del techo es una estructura en forma de V y en acero hueco del que parten unas vigas también de acero que sujetan el techo de vidrio.

La straordinaria copertura in vetro, legno e acciaio fa affluire luce solare nella stazione, creando un'atmosfera accogliente per i viaggiatori. È costituita da una serie di elementi continui dalla sezione a "V" capovolta, da cui si dipartono, su entrambi i lati, dei bracci in acciaio che sorreggono la struttura in vetro.

FLORENCE STATION
FLORENCE

Still under design and construction by architects Foster + Partners, the Florence TAV Station will meld the new technology of high-speed transit with the classical architecture of the city surrounding it. Connected via escalators and elevators, the station platform resides entirely underground. An arrival at street level is greeted with a flood of natural light and a terrace made to overlook the bustling station below.

Der TAV-Bahnhof in Florenz, der noch von den Architekten Foster + Partners erbaut wird, soll die neue Technologie der Hochgeschwindigkeitszüge mit der klassischen Architektur der Stadt in Einklang bringen. Verbunden durch Lifte und Rolltreppen befinden sich die Bahnsteige alle unter der Erde. Wenn man auf der Straßenebene auftaucht, wird man von natürlichem Tageslicht und einer Plattform begrüßt, von der aus man den geschäftigen Bahnhof darunter beobachten kann.

Conçue par les architectes Foster + Partners, la gare TAV de Florence combinera une technologie de pointe de transit de grande vitesse avec l'architecture classique de la ville environnante. Connectée grâce à des escaliers roulants et des ascenceurs, la plate-forme de la gare est entièrement souterraine. Une sortie sur la rue permettra de faire rentrer la lumière naturelle et une terrasse donnaera sur l'animation de la gare.

Este proyecto, aún se encuentra en fase de construcción y diseño de la mano de los arquitectos Foster + Partners. La estación de TAV de Florencia realiza una perfecta fusión entre la tecnología de la alta velocidad y la arquitectura clásica de la ciudad que la rodea. Conectada por ascensores y escaleras automáticas, los andenes se encuentran en la parte subterránea de la estación. Está previsto que la entrada, a la altura de la calle, reciba un torrente de luz natural y que una terraza ofrezca vistas a la animada estación.

Tuttora in fase di progettazione e costruzione da parte dello studio Foster + Partners, la stazione TAV di Firenze si prefigge di coniugare la nuova tecnologia dell'alta velocità con la classica architettura cittadina circostante. Raggiungibili con ascensori e scale mobili, i binari della stazione saranno completamente sotterranei. L'ingresso al livello stradale, inondato di luce naturale, proseguirà in una terrazza pensata per dominare dall'alto l'andirivieni di treni e passeggeri.

Between the platform level and the street are two levels of shops, while a terrace at street level offers a view over the tracks and trains arriving and departing.

Zwischen Gleis- und Straßenebene liegen zwei Geschäftsetagen, während eine Terrasse auf Höhe der Straße den Blick auf die Gleise und die ein- und ausfahrenden Züge ermöglicht.

Entre le niveau d'arrivée et la rue, il y a deux niveaux des magasins, alors qu'une terrasse au niveau rue offre une vue sur les voies et l'arrivée et le départ des trains.

Entre los subterráneos donde se encuentran los andenes y la calle hay dos niveles más con comercios. La terraza, que se encuentra al nivel de la calle, ofrece una vista sobre las vías y la entrada y salida de los trenes.

Tra il livello stradale e quello dei binari sono previsti due piani di negozi, mentre da una terrazza al piano terra si potrà godere della vista dei binari con i treni in arrivo e in partenza.

Passengers move from platform to ground level via elevators or escalators.

Mit Aufzügen und Rolltreppen gelangen die Passagiere von den Bahnsteigen an die Oberfläche.

Les passagers se déplacent du niveau d'arrivée au niveau chaussée à l'aide d'ascenseurs ou d'escalators.

Los pasajeros se desplazan desde los andenes hasta la planta baja mediante ascensores y escaleras mecánicas.

I passeggeri si sposteranno dai binari al piano terra usando scale mobili e ascensori.

KAZANSKY STATION
MOSCOW

As one of the most architectually-rich stations in the world, the Kazansky Station is built in a Neo Russian motif by Russian architect, Aleksej Shusev. Originally having only minimal railroad lines, the station today links Moscow to Povolzhie, the Urals, Siberia, and Middle Asia. Reminiscent of Suumbeck tower in Kazan Kremlin, the station bares an ancient Russian influence illustrated by the tiered turret over the central entrance. Famous artists such as Benua, Kustodiev, and Rerikh contributed to both the interior and exterior decor of the station making it an artistic masterpiece.

Der Kasaner Bahnhof gehört zu den architektonisch üppigsten Bahnhöfen der Welt. Er wurde im neorussischen Stil von dem russischen Architekten Aleksej Shusev konzipiert. Ursprünglich nur mit wenigen Gleisen versehen, verbindet der Bahnhof heute Moskau mit Povolzhie, dem Ural, Sibirien und Zentralasien. Der Bahnhof erinnert an den Sujumbike-Turm des Kasaner Kreml und knüpft an altrussische Stile an, die sich z. B. in dem zweistufigen Türmchen über dem Haupteingang widerspiegeln. Berühmte Künstler wie Benua, Kustodiev, und Rerikh trugen sowohl zum Inneren als auch Äußeren des Bahnhofs bei und machten ihn zu einem künstlerischen Meisterwerk.

Considérée comme une des gares les plus complexes à niveau architectural du monde, la gare Kazansky est construite dans un style néo-russe par l'architecte russe, Aleksej Shusev. Dotée du minimum de lignes ferroviaires à l'origine, la gare relie aujourd'hui Moscou à Povolzhie, l'Oural, la Sibérie et l'Asie mineure. Réminiscence de la tour Söyembikä du Kremlin Kazan, la gare est marquée par l'influence de l'ancienne Russie illustrée par la tour de l'entrée centrale. Des artistes réputés comme Benua, Kustodiev et Rerikh ont contribué à faire du décor intérieur et extérieur un chef d'œuvre artistique.

La estación Kazansky, construida con motivos neorusos por el arquitecto ruso Aleksej Shusev, es arquitectónicamente hablando una de las más ricas del mundo. Antiguamente era una estación dedicada a trayectos cortos. Hoy día enlaza Moscú con Povolzhie, los Urales, Siberia y Asia central. La estación recuerda a la torre Suumbeck en Kazan Kremlin y denota una gran influencia de la antigua Rusia, ilustrada por el torreón en la entrada principal. Artistas famosos como Benua, Kustodiev y Rerikh contribuyeron a la decoración interior y exterior de la estación convirtiéndola en una artística pieza maestra.

Tra le stazioni più architettonicamente ricche del mondo, la stazione Kazanskij fu costruita in stile neorusso dall'architetto Aleksej Shusev. Quella da cui un tempo partivano solo poche linee, oggi collega Mosca alla regione del Volga, agli Urali, alla Siberia e all'Asia Minore. Ispirata alla torre Söyembikä del cremlino di Kazan', la stazione tradisce le influenze della Russia antica per esempio nella torretta a più livelli che domina l'ingresso principale. Con i suoi arredi interni ed esterni opera di artisti quali Benua, Kustodiev e Rerikh, la stazione Kazanskij si configura come un vero e proprio tesoro d'arte.

LEGENDARY TRAINS

LEGENDARY TRAINS

The 1920s and 1930s were the golden age of rail. The wealthy lavished their fortunes on touring in these iron giants, these palaces on wheels. Our memories of these travels are wrapped in a glow of romanticism and mystery, not in vanity—a part of our history was written in these carriages; they have housed spies, presidents, and even royalty. The story of train travel was interrupted by the Second World War but that has been repaired as the 1970s saw a resurgence and renovation of these legendary trains to all their past splendor.

Die 20er und 30er Jahre waren das goldene Zeitalter der Züge. Die Reichen benutzten ihr Vermögen dazu, in diesen eisernen Giganten, diesen „Palästen auf Rädern" zu reisen. Unsere Erinnerungen an diese Reisen sind von romantisch geheimnisvollen Vorstellungen geprägt und das nicht ohne Grund. Ein Teil unserer Geschichte wurde in diesen Wagen geschrieben, denn hier hielten sich Spione, Präsidenten und sogar Könige auf. Die Geschichte der Luxuszugfahrten wurde durch den Zweiten Weltkrieg unterbrochen, aber seit den 70er Jahren wird mit neuem Elan und Erfindungsreichtum an die frühere Pracht angeknüpft.

Les années 20 et 30 sont considérées comme l'âge d'or du rail. Les gens fortunés dépensaient leur argent en faisant du tourisme dans ces géants de fer, ces « palais sur roues ». Les souvenirs associés à ces voyages sont recouverts d'un voile de romantisme et de mystère, non de vanité – une partie de notre histoire a été écrite dans ces wagons, y ont été logés espions, présidents et même la royauté. L'histoire du voyage en train fut interrompue par la deuxième Guerre Mondiale, mais les années 1970 ont vu la résurgence et la rénovation de ces trains légendaires dans toute leur splendeur d'antan.

Los años 20 y 30 del siglo pasado fueron los años dorados del tren. Millonarios de todo el mundo derrochaban sus fortunas recorriendo los caminos de hierro en auténticos "palacios sobre ruedas". En nuestra memoria permanecen envueltos en un halo de romanticismo y misterio, no en vano, parte de la Historia se ha escrito en esos vagones, que acogieron a la realeza, a presidentes y a espías. Esta historia quedó interrumpida por la Segunda Guerra Mundial, pero se ha ido recuperando a partir de los años 70 restaurando o reproduciendo los trenes legendarios de antaño en todo su esplendor.

Gli anni venti e trenta del secolo scorso sono stati l'epoca d'oro della ferrovia. I ricchi dilapidavano le loro fortune viaggiando a bordo di questi giganti d'acciaio, veri e propri "palazzi su ruote". I nostri ricordi di quei viaggi sono però avvolti in un alone di romanticismo e mistero, non di vanità: su quelle carrozze è stata scritta parte della nostra storia, quei convogli hanno ospitato spie, capi di stato, monarchi. La storia dei viaggi ferroviari si interrompe momentaneamente con la Seconda guerra mondiale, uno strappo ricucito negli anni settanta quando questi treni leggendari tornano in auge recuperando lo splendore di un tempo.

Swedish Royal Train

A second class passenger car from 1902 of the local railway Utrecht – Baarn – Zwolle, a region in the Netherlands inhabited by relatively rich residents. Image from The National Railway Museum in the Netherlands.

Ein Zweiter-Klasse-Wagen aus dem Jahr 1902 der Lokalbahn Utrecht – Baarn – Zwolle, einer Region in den Niederlanden mit einer relativ wohlhabenden Bevölkerung. Bild vom Nationalen Eisenbahnmuseum der Niederlande.

Passager de deuxième classe en 1902 du chemin de fer local d'Utrecht – Baarn – Zwolle, une région aux Pays-Bas habitée par des résidents relativement riches. Image du Musée du Chemin de fer national des Pays-Bas.

Vagón de pasajeros de segunda clase de 1902 del ferrocarril local de Utrecht – Baarn – Zwolle, una región en Holanda con una población relativamente rica. Imagen procedente del Museo Nacional Ferroviario en Holanda.

Vettura passeggeri di seconda classe del 1902 destinata al trasporto locale sulla tratta Utrecht – Baarn – Zwolle, in una regione d'Olanda relativamente facoltosa. Immagine fornita dal Museo Nazionale delle Ferrovie dei Paesi Bassi.

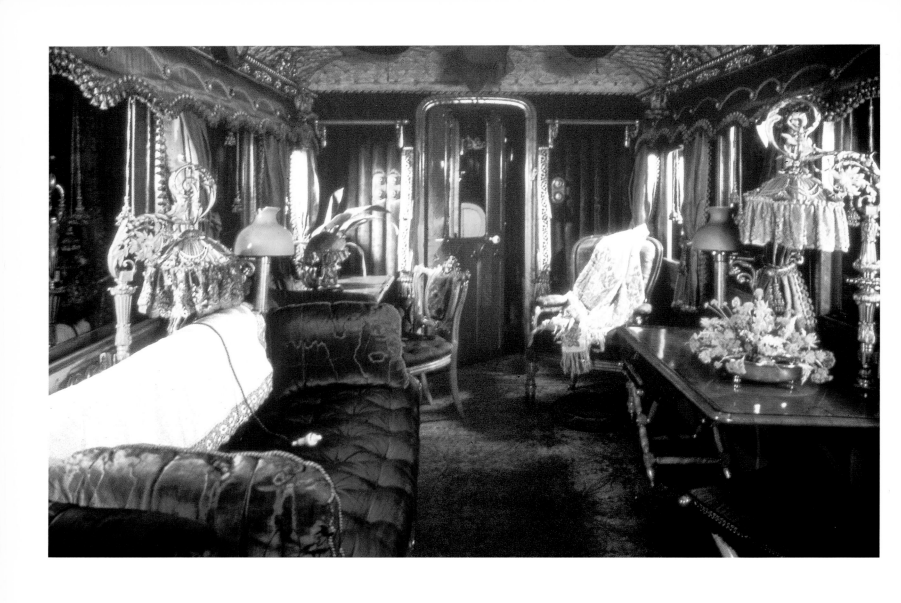

Tableau of Queen Victoria sitting in the royal carriage built for her by the London & North Western Railway with her lady-in-waiting. On June 13, 1842, Queen Victoria became the first British monarch to travel by train.

Darstellung von Königin Victoria und einer Gesellschafterin im königlichen Eisenbahnwagen, der für sie von der Bahngesellschaft London & North Western erbaut wurde. Als erste britische Monarchin reiste sie am 13. Juni 1842 mit dem Zug.

Tableau de la Reine Victoria et de sa dame de compagnie assises dans le wagon royal construit pour elle par le London & North Western Railway. Le 13 juin 1842, la Reine Victoria devient le premier monarque britannique à voyager en train.

Cuadro de la reina Victoria y su dama de compañía sentadas en el vagón real, construido especialmente para ella por el London & North Western Railway. El 13 de junio de 1842 la reina Victoria se convirtió en la primera monarca británica que viajó en tren.

Raffigurazione della regina Vittoria seduta con la dama di compagnia nella carrozza reale appositamente costruita per lei dalla London & North Western Railway. Il 13 giugno 1842 la regina Vittoria divenne il primo monarca inglese a viaggiare a bordo di un treno.

The Al Andalus Express began traveling to Andalusia starting in 1985 and took this classic route to Al Andalus until its disappearance in 2005. The décor of this train, one of the most luxurious in the world, emulated the style of the "Orient Express."

Der Al Andalus Express fuhr ab 1985 auf der klassischen Route nach Andalusien, bis er 2005 abgeschafft wurde. Die Ausstattung des Zuges, einer der luxuriösesten der Welt, ahmte den Stil des „Orient Express" nach.

L'Al Andalus Express initie ses voyages en partance d'Andalousie en 1985 et emprunte le fameux trajet vers Al Andalus jusqu'à sa disparition en 2005. Le décor de ce train, un des plus luxueux du monde, est inspiré par le style de l'Orient Express.

Los coches del Al Andalus Expreso empezaron a rodar por Andalucia a partir de 1985 y realizaron esta ruta clásica por el Al Andalus hasta su desaparición en 2005. La decoración de este tren, uno de los más lujosos del mundo, emulaba el estilo del "Orient Express".

L'Al Andalus Expreso ha inaugurato la classica tratta per l'Andalusia nel 1985, mantenendo il servizio fino al 2005. L'arredo del treno, uno dei più lussuosi del mondo, era ispirato allo stile dell'Orient Express.

Winston Churchill (above) and Princess Elizabeth and the Duke of Edinburgh (left) are among some of the notable figures in history that have traveled aboard the Royal Canadian Pacific's fleet.

Winston Churchill (oben), Prinzessin Elizabeth und der Herzog von Edinburgh (links) gehören zu den berühmtesten Persönlichkeiten der Geschichte, die mit dem Royal Canadian Pacific reisten.

Winston Churchill (ci-dessus), la Princesse Elizabeth et le Duc d'Édimbourg (à gauche) sont parmi les figures les plus importantes de l'histoire ayant voyagé à bord du Royal Canadian Pacific.

Winston Churchill (arriba) y la princesa Elizabeth, y el duque de Edimburgo (izquierda) son algunas de las figuras relevantes de la historia que viajaron a bordo del Royal Canadian Pacific.

Winston Churchill (sopra), la principessa Elisabetta e il duca di Edimburgo (sinistra) sono tra i più illustri personaggi storici ad aver viaggiato a bordo della flotta della Royal Canadian Pacific.

Glacier Express near Samedan, Celerina, about 1930

Glacier Express in der Nähe von Samedan/Celerina, um 1930

Glacier Express prés de Samedan à Celerina, aux environs de 1930

Glacier Express cerca a Samedan, Celerina, por los años 1930

Il Glacier Express vicino a Samedan, Celerina, intorno al 1930

The Queen Mother welcoming her daughter Princess Elizabeth (Later Queen Elizabeth II), at Euston Station on her return from her American tour. The Duke of Edinburgh is stepping out of the train and a young Prince Charles stands nearby in front of Princess Margaret.

Die Königin Mutter begrüßt ihre Tochter Prinzessin Elizabeth (die spätere Königin Elizabeth II.) an der Euston Station bei ihrer Rückkehr aus den USA. Der Herzog von Edinburgh verlässt gerade den Zug, während ein junger Prinz Charles und Prinzessin Margaret auf dem Bahnsteig warten.

La Reine-mère accueillant la Princesse sa fille Elizabeth (la future Reine Elizabeth II), à Euston Station à son retour des États-Unis. Le Duc d'Édimbourg sur le quai accompagné du jeune Prince Charles se tenant debout à proximité de la Princesse Margaret.

La Reina Madre dando la bienvenida a su hija la Princesa Elizabeth (posteriormente la Reina Elizabeth II), en Euston Station a su regreso de su tour americano. El Duque de Edimburgo saliendo del tren y el joven Príncipe Carlos delante de la Princesa Margaret.

Alla Euston Station la Regina Madre accoglie sua figlia, la principessa Elisabetta (futura regina Elisabetta II) di ritorno da un viaggio in America. Si vede il duca di Edimburgo scendere dal treno mentre il bambino in piedi davanti alla principessa Margaret è il principe Carlo.

PARIS
GOLDEN
ARROW

Daily
Pullman
Service
from
London
Victoria

Tickets and reservations
from principal Travel Agencies
or Continental Enquiry Office
Victoria Station London SW1

SOUTHERN
BRITISH RAILWAYS

The Super Chief

The Super Chief, often referred to as "The Train of the Stars" because of the numerous celebrities that traveled on the streamliner between Chicago and Los Angeles, set a new standard for luxury rail in America when it made its first run from Dearborn Station in Chicago on May 12, 1936.

Der Super Chief, den man wegen der zahlreichen Berühmtheiten, die zwischen Chicago und Los Angeles bereits mit ihm reisten, auch den „Zug der Stars" nennt, setzte in den USA neue Maßstäbe für Luxuszüge, als er zum ersten Mal am 12. Mai 1936 von der Dearborn Station in Chicago losfuhr.

Le Super Chief, souvent connu sous le nom du « Train des Stars » en raison des nombreuses célébrités ayant voyagé sur la ligne Chicago – Los Angeles, a mis en place un nouveau standing pour les lignes ferroviaires de luxe aux États-Unis lors de son premier parcours en partance de Dearborn Station à Chicago le 12 mai 1936.

El Super Chief, apodado "el tren de las estrellas" por las numerosas celebridades que viajaron de Chicago a Los Ángeles en este tren aerodinámico, marcó un nuevo estándar en los trenes de lujo en América desde que realizó su primer trayecto desde Dearborn Station, Chicago, el 12 de Mayo de 1936.

L'aerodinamico Super Chief, spesso chiamato il "treno delle star" a cause delle numerose celebrità che se ne sono servite per viaggiare tra Chicago e Los Angeles, introdusse in America un nuovo standard di lusso ferroviario in occasione del suo primo viaggio dalla Dearborn Station di Chicago il 12 maggio 1936.

This page on the left, the salon coach belonging to the last German Empress Augusta Victoria, wife of Emperor Wilhelm; this car was built in 1911 in Breslau. More or less coaches were used depending on how many they needed for the trip. Since 1917, a sleeper car was transformed to put up a telegraph service. On the right, an image of the Talgo.

Auf dieser Seite links der Salonwagen der letzten deutschen Kaiserin, Augusta Viktoria, der Gemahlin Kaiser Wilhelms II.; dieser Wagon wurde 1911 in Breslau erbaut. Je nach Bedarf hängte man für eine Reise entweder mehr oder weniger Wagen an. Ab 1917 wurde ein Schlafwagen in einen Telegraphenwagon umgebaut. Rechts ein Bild des Talgo.

Page gauche, le wagon salon ayant appartenu à la dernière impératrice allemande Augusta Victoria, épouse de l'empereur Wilhelm ; cette voiture a été construite en 1911 à Breslau. Plus ou moins de wagons furent utilisés selon la nécessité du voyage. Depuis 1917, une voiture lit fut transformée pour installer un service de télégraphe. Du côté droit, une photo du Talgo.

En esta página a la izquierda, el vagón salón perteneciente a la última emperatriz alemana, Augusta Victoria, esposa del emperador Guillermo II. Este vagón fue construido en 1911 en Breslau. Dependiendo de las necesidades de cada viaje se añadían más o menos vagones al tren. En 1917, un coche-cama fue transformado en servicio telegráfico. A la derecha, una imagen del Talgo.

Su questa pagina a sinistra la carrozza salone dell'ultima imperatrice tedesca Augusta Vittoria, moglie dell'imperatore Guglielmo II; questa vettura fu costruita nel 1911 a Breslau. Il numero di carrozze variava a seconda delle necessità del viaggio. Nel 1917 un vagone letto fu trasformato per ospitare un servizio di telegrafo. A destra un'immagine del Talgo.

This picture of the Kaiser Wilhelm Train was taken in 1894. The train had nine cars that housed the emperor and empress' salon, the luggage car, the pantry, the kitchen and the spaces reserved for the retinue.

Diese Fotografie des Kaiser-Wilhelm-Zuges stammt aus dem Jahr 1894. Der Zug hatte neun Wagons, zu denen der kaiserliche Salonwagen, der Gepäckwagen, die Speisekammer, der Küchenwagen und ein Wagen für die Dienerschaft gehörte.

Photographie du train du Kaiser Wilhelm prise en 1894. Le train compte neuf wagons, hébergeant le salon de l'empereur et de l'impératrice, l'équipage, les provisions, la cuisine et les espaces réservés à la suite.

Imagen del tren del Kaiser Wilhelm tomada en 1894. El tren contaba con 9 vagones, que albergaban el salón del emperador y la emperatriz, el equipaje, la despensa, la cocina y los espacios reservados al séquito.

Fotografia del treno Kaiser Wilhelm scattata nel 1894. Il convoglio era composto da nove vagoni comprendenti il salotto dell'imperatore e dell'imperatrice, la carrozza bagagli, la dispensa, la cucina e gli spazi riservati al seguito imperiale.

In 1952, the first Talgo II became the pioneer in Talgo commercial train services.

Der erste Talgo II aus dem Jahr 1952 wurde zum Pionier des kommerziellen Talgo-Fahrgastbetriebs.

En 1952, le premier Talgo II fut le pionnier des services commerciaux de train Talgo.

En 1952, el primer Talgo II se convirtió en el pionero de los trenes con servicio comercial.

Nel 1952 il primo Talgo II fu il pioniere del trasporto persone effettuato dai treni Talgo.

Photo Credits

Arcadis: 181 – 185 (Michel Kievits).
Archivo fotográfico ADIF: 204 – 205.
Blue Train: 7, 59 – 61. Courtesy of Blue Train.
California State Railroad Museum: 212 – 215.
DB AG: 117 (Max Lautenschläger), 118 (Stefan Klarner), 119 (Hierl), 152 and 155 (Christian Bedeschinski),157 (Hartmut Reiche), 158 – 159 (Horn), 160 – 161 (Andreas Muhs).
DB Museum Nürnberg: 216 (right), 217.
Foster + Partners: 187 – 191.
Frederik Tellerup: 122 – 123.
Golden Chariot: © The Luxury Trains 81 – 85.
GrandLuxe: 55 and back cover top left (Bruce Fleming), 56 (GrandLuxe rail journeys), 57 (Robert Knight).
GW Travel Limited: 9, 87 – 91, 93 – 95, 193 – 195.
Majestic Imperator: 51 – 53, 142.
Orient Express: 19, 21, 22, 25, 26, 27, 29 (JP Masclet), 30, 31, 33 (Kan Sakurai), 35, 36 – 37 (Giles Christopher), 39 (Ian Lloyd), 40 (Bottom: Willy Tang), 41, 138 (Giles Christopher), 141, 146, 148 (Ryan Davies), 149 (Ian Lloyd), 150 (JP Masclet), 151.
Renfe Operadora AVE: 99, 125, 126, 127, 128 – 129 and back cover bottom left (Patier).
Rhätische Bahn AG and Matterhorn Gotthard Bahn: 131, 132 (top and middle).
Rhätische Bahn AG: 15 (Andrea Badrutt), 132 (bottom: Andrea Badrutt), 208 (Albert Steiner).
Rovos Rail: © 2007, 2008. Courtesy of Rovos Rail Tours (Pty) Ltd.: 16 and back cover top right, 63 – 69, 144.
Royal Canadian Pacific: 11, 75, 76, 77, 78 (Top: Bilodeau – Preston; bottom: Rick Roinson/CPR), 79, 143, 145 and 147 (Rick Roinson/CPR), 206 and 207 (Courtesy of Canadian Pacific Archives).
Shinkansen: 113 – 115. Courtesy of Central Japan Railway Company.
SJ: 121(Kasper Dudzik).
SNCF Médiathèque: 96, 101, 102 – 103 (Sylvain Cambon), 104 (Christophe Recoura), 105 (top: Bernard Lachaud; bottom: Christophe Recoura),106 – 111, 163 (Christophe Recoura), 164 (bottom), 165 (Christophe Recoura), 171 – 173 (Jean-Marc Fabro).
Grimshaw: 175 and 178 (Shannon McGrath); 176 – 177 and 179 (John Gollings).
Swedish Railway Museum: 196, 199 and cover (Hans Blomberg).
Talgo: 216 (right), 218, 219.
Tangula Luxury trains: 135 – 137. Courtesy of Tangula Luxury trains.
The National Railway Museum in The Netherlands: 200, 201.
The National Railway Museum (UK)/Science & Society Picture Library: 202, 203, 209 – 211.
Thomas Groussin: 164 (top).
Train Bleu Restaurant: 13, 166 – 167, 168 – 169 and back cover bottom right (Arnaud Frich).
Luxury Train Travel: 34 – 35. Courtesy Trainchatering/Orient Express.
El Transcantábrico – FEVE: 43 – 49.
Victoria hotels & resorts: 71 – 73.